POLITICAL BEHAVIORALISM
AND
MODERN JURISPRUDENCE

POLITICAL BEHAVIORALISM

AND

MODERN JURISPRUDENCE:

A Working Theory and Study in Judicial Decision-Making

THEODORE L. BECKER

University of Hawaii

Rand McNally & Company   Chicago

126650

RAND McNALLY PUBLIC AFFAIRS SERIES

America Armed: Essays on United States Military Policy
A Nation of States: Essays on the American Federal System
Why Foreign Aid?
Political Parties, U.S.A.
100 Years of Emancipation

RAND McNALLY POLITICAL SCIENCE SERIES

BECKER, Political Behavioralism and Modern Jurisprudence
BOBROW, ed., Components of Defense Policy
ELDERSVELD, Political Parties: A Behavioral Analysis
FROMAN, Congressmen and Their Constituencies
GOLEMBIEWSKI, Behavior and Organization: O & M and the Small Group
HAIGHT and JOHNSTON, eds., The President: Roles and Powers
HANNA, ed., Independent Black Africa
LONG, The Polity
MILBRATH, Political Participation: How and Why Do People Get Involved in Politics?
The Washington Lobbyists
PEABODY and POLSBY, eds., New Perspectives on the House of Representatives
SCHMIDHAUSER, ed., Constitutional Law in the Political Process
SINGER, ed., Human Behavior and International Politics: Contributions from the Social-Psychological Sciences
SCHUBERT, ed., Judicial Behavior: A Reader in Theory and Research
STRAUSS, The City and Man
STRAUSS and CROPSEY, eds., History of Political Philosophy
ULMER, ed., Introductory Reader in Political Behavior
WILLIAMS and PRESS, eds., Democracy in Urban America: Readings in Government and Politics

Preface

HOPEFULLY, this study, generated from the friction of highly polarized viewpoints, is the first of many steps directed towards satisfying a long-standing curiosity. Specifically, it is an attempt to establish a way to find out what makes the appellate judicial mind operate as it does. That is, of course, if we can really say that the mental operations of the appellate judge are any different from those of the rest of us, or from the rest of those whom we perceive as policy-makers.

During the winter of 1961, Professor Victor G. Rosenblum of Northwestern University conducted an interesting series of Sunday morning seminars in his home as a supplement to his Law and Politics graduate course. On one of these occasions, the good professor moderated a particularly heated debate between me and my peers regarding the nature of the judiciary. The others held that judges were merely legislators in black robes whereas I, being a law school lawyer, disagreed with their convictions. Furthermore, they insisted that the judge (particularly in the appellate courts) simply rationalized his own subjectively derived opinion in fancy, esoteric, "objective" terminology.

Professor Rosenblum artfully engendered enough discord to make this basic issue the main theme of that winter's sabbath sessions. As a (non-practicing) lawyer, I felt obliged to defend the bench against an unwarranted assault by attempting to enlighten my lay friends. "You just can't appreciate the judicial temperament," I'd stammer. However, the arguments both pro and con were appalling since they were founded far more on value judgments than upon facts. Probably no one participant managed to convince any of the others. Indeed, I hardly managed to convince myself that we had even sufficiently delineated the issue. At the time, it was an acutely frustrating set of experiences for me. Yet, an energy was created that prompted an attempt to employ some available resources and tools in order to satisfy myself as to whether or not the judicial process does indeed have a certain effective uniqueness.

To accomplish this, several steps had to be taken. First, a comprehensive, detailed study had to be undertaken of the work of the many trained observers of the judicial process. From their thoughts, key factors had to be sifted out and set apart. What are the major theoretical parts in this specific thought process which we call the appellate judicial process? This was the key question which had to be answered before a model could be developed to guide any study of the actual dynamics of any such process. Then, of course, hypotheses had to be framed and operations conceived and carried out.

It is not surprising, considering this writer's training in the law and in the behavioral approach to political science, that this type of work should result (particularly under the catalytic heat supplied by those Sunday episodes). Thus, what follows is a social scientific examination of the nature and dynamics of what is conceived by all jurisprudents and some political scientists to be the major distinguishing features of the appellate judicial process, i.e., the impact of the existence of a body of legal precedent, in interaction with the role demand of *stare decisis* in a litigation appeal context, on the outcome of that process: the judicial decision.

I sincerely hope that what follows is an objective, systematic and rigorous study of the problem. I also hope that the tentativeness of the notion of "working theory" in the subtitle is borne in mind. After all, in my view, the following work can only be a beginning, a preface, as it were, to much needed research in a still much too mysterious field of study. In the words of Herman Melville:

> . . . I hereupon offer my own poor endeavors. I promise nothing complete; because any human thing supposed to be complete, must for that very reason infallibly be faulty . . . But I now leave my cetological system standing thus unfinished, even as the great Cathedral of Cologne was left, with the crane still standing upon the top of the uncompleted tower. For small erections may be finished by their first architects; grand ones, true ones, ever leave the copestone to posterity. God keep me from ever completing anything. This whole book is but a draft —nay, but the draft of a draft. Oh, Time, Strength, Cash, and Patience!

Detroit, Michigan; March, 1964
Honolulu, Hawaii; November, 1964   T.L.B.

Contents

List of Tables

Acknowledgments

THE debt owed to the many friends and associates who assisted me materially and emotionally in completing this work is great. Many of them know that simple words on paper can never begin to repay their kindnesses. All are now put on official notice that the inclusion of their name below signifies a recognition on my part of the crucial nature of their necessary and sufficient support of my work.

First, much is owed to my primary intellectual developers, prodders, and encouragers: Victor G. Rosenblum, Richard D. Schwartz, and C. Willard Heckel. Those from whom I have learned much or upon whom I have relied for moral support during critical times in the lengthy development of this work include: Thornton H. Anderson, Richard and Paula Becker, Karen Black, Richard A. Brody, Donald T. Campbell, William Caspary, Karen Curtis, Richard E. Dawson, William G. Fleming, Harold M. Herman, Edward and Jackie Heubel, Adam Przeworski, James A. Robinson, Baljit Singh, Nat and Lorena Simons, Gary N. Skoloff, and Norman Wengert.

I also owe much to those who spent a good deal of time and effort in more professional contributions to this study: first and foremost is Donald C. Hildum who must be singled out for his essential assistance; in fact, one might say that his help was of statistically significant proportions. Other important contributors and assistors are Sheldon Appleton, Lionel Frankel, Robert Harris, Gerald Israel, Richard Miller, and Samuel Shuman. Gratitude is also extended to Roger Cunningham, Byron Higgins, Robert Howes, Charles Schutz, Carl Vann, and Glen Weston for lending me their classes, and to Robert S. Cahill, Marianne Clark, David J. Danelski, and Joel B. Grossman for their comments and suggestions on the manuscript.

But, perhaps most of all—in satisfying my own personal desire to locate and acknowledge unmoved movers and good fortune—I must thank two people who made two key choices some six years ago. One of these I never knew or met, yet had he not declined an offer of a graduate assistantship at the University of Maryland in April, 1958, this work probably would never have had its start. Similarly, had my former wife not decided to give up much of what she actually could not afford to give for two long years, this work would never have come to pass. I dedicate this work to her and a small group of dear friends mentioned above, with deepest and enduring affection; To R.M., G.N.S., both Karens, and the Alpha Dirties, and their several associates.

Rulers will find considerable doses of falsehood and deceit necessary for the good of their subjects.

Plato

On the whole, it is desirable that this ideal respect for law, although it rests ultimately on a mistake which the shrewd do not make—belief in the omnipotence of law—be developed as far as possible, that it become a sort of religion because of the resulting tranquility and economy of social forces.

René Demogue

It does justice good to be administered in the open; the wind blows her skirts up and you can see what she's got underneath.

Bertolt Brecht

A fuller understanding of legal method has been retarded because it has rarely been explored for the simple purpose of learning the truth about it. . . . In any event, one of the most important questions of legal method, the central issue in the recent debates, concerns the role of legal rules in the process of adjudication.

Jerome Hall

Introduction

THE billboard blared: "Impeach Earl Warren!" Its simple and sharp (red, white, and blue, mostly red) message erupted into view and caused an immediate feeling of dismay within me. I began to mutter profanities against the signboard. But then it occurred to me that this particular sign's content shouldn't have been so surprising or so dismaying. The shock I experienced was probably due more to its sudden appearance, and the dismay to its advertising agency brashness. After all, I knew that the United States Supreme Court as an institution and several of its individual members have come under extremely heavy political pressures in the last three decades. From court packing schemes to numerous proposed congressional bills and constitutional amendments, from being called the "nine old men" and the "Communist Court"—the highest tribunal in our land has been threatened with assault and has been the object of much vituperation. Like it or not, the Court and the courts have become openly involved in major politics—and they, in turn, have become fair political game. In fact, in 1964, we even found the Republican candidate for the Presidency telling Southerners that he would select justices who were more favorable to the South than those chosen by previous Presidents. It has come to that!

So the courts are deeply involved in politics and actually have been for some time. But long before the popular awareness of this fact, various American scholars in the law schools, the courts themselves, and the colleges saw, described, and sought to understand the court-politics interrelationship. The still fecund legal realist movement in American jurisprudence and the judicial behavioral movement in American political science began, in turn, to write of the relationship of courts to politics and particularly of the Supreme Court's commitment in the American political arena.

This book has not been written to further or add to the tracts and pamphlets which either extol or damn court participation in the political system. The shrill denunciations of the Supreme Court's supposed usurpation of power are simply cries of men whose toes have been stomped on, or of men who will say anything which seems to gain them political advantage. Their analysis, if it can be called that, comes through maddened eyes. Though in the long run their view that various actions of the courts or the Supreme Court are novel and bad and ought to be stopped may yet prove to be correct in a functional sense, their cries should now only serve to awaken more people to that which needs be studied. And that is what this book is all about. Its interest lies with those who are involved in *learning* and *understanding* rather than in advancing their own special interests. Its specific interest is with advancing as best it can the study of the common-law appellate decision-making process— that process of which the United States Supreme Court is but one small part.

It is the writer's view that, although the two groups of analysts mentioned above have contributed much to the study of appellate decision-making, there has been somewhat too much duplication and misdirection of energy, time, and financial resources in the work done. Thus far, only the barest foundation has been laid for systematic and rigorous study of what is at least theorized to be the distinctive appellate judicial process. The political scientists appear to have been often tangential to and almost always without hint of any theoretical link to the main problem. The legal scholars, it will also be shown, have been much too sweeping and vague. In other words, the increase in degree of understanding of this theoretically distinctive process has not been nearly proportional to the increase of interest in it.

As long as such a situation continues, this book, despite the fact that its analysis is based on research conducted during and before 1964, will not become outdated. The political scientists have stated explicitly and implicitly that they are studying the judicial process as a behavioral system. They state that they are attempting to *understand* the judge as a behaving organism as the key to understanding that process, and possibly to explaining variances in patterns of judicial decisions. The first chapter attempts to point out that they have not advanced too far in that undertaking which they themselves have defined— and that, as they are going in the main, they stand to gain little further ground. Of course the critical portions of the first chapter do not include and are not meant to include the full range of potential criticism directable at the work of the political science judicial behavioralists to date. In fact both the writer and Professor Wallace Mendelson have recently appraised this body of work from somewhat different approaches.[1] *The criticism which follows is related directly to a plan to suggest a remedy for the faults found and described.* In this study, notions of what has been most wrong in the work thus far done will go hand in hand with notions of what actually must be done if we are to achieve the ultimate goals established by all judicial behavioralists, including those whose work will be examined below. One word of optimism, since all is not as gloomy as might be inferred from the above statements. For there are highly encouraging signs that real progress is at hand. The work which is responsible for this encouragement is also reviewed and discussed.

The second chapter is also a review of a body of literature. Legal scholars, jurisprudents, and judges have frequently examined and theorized upon the judicial decision-making process from the perspective of its being a unique human thinking process directly related to judicial decision-making behavior. Many

---

[1] Wallace Mendelson, "The Neo-Behavioral Approach to the Judicial Process: A Critique," *American Political Science Review,* 57 (Sept., 1963), 593–603; Theodore L. Becker, "Inquiry into a School of Thought in the Judicial Behavior Movement," *Midwest Journal of Political Science,* 7 (Aug., 1963), 254–66.

of these men have studied that which they believe to be a distinctive thought process factor as an aspect of the entire process which affects the ultimate decision. However, it is rare that their work is done in the rigorous, descriptive manner which characterizes that done by the political behavioralists. Rather to the contrary, the legal scholars often set the concept of judicial role in a *normative* context. This, though of great importance, does not significantly help in understanding the *actual* relationship between the process and the policy; nor does it even help much in describing the real nature of judicial role. However since they have also studied the intricacies of the process so carefully, their work becomes a body of material which we can draw upon for our purposes.

Although one of the major concepts employed in the studies of the jurisprudents is that of role, or judicial role, the jurisprudents' use of this concept is somewhat different from its use by social scientists. Role is not defined by the jurisprudents in terms of overt, empirical behavior expectations, but rather in terms of a desired type of decision-making or thinking process. It is an exhortation (normative) to the occupant of the position of the judge. The third chapter is partially devoted to a more detailed examination of some of the problems involved in the use of the concept of role.

Hopefully, the purpose of this book is to wed the best of the two approaches, i.e., that of the political behavioralists and that of the legal scholars, in an attempt to advance toward a sound, empirically verifiable theory of judicial decision-making. Ultimately, we are interested in describing the relationship (if any exists) between the judicial decision-making role with other key variables, and with the ultimate outcome of the judicial process. We must in some way discover the nature and trace the effect, if any, of the decision-making role variable upon the judicial decision. I personally believe that there *is* a definite, significant effect. If this belief is correct, and can be at least partially demonstrated below, then this work will have contributed toward (1) an understanding of the nature of the judicial process by assisting in the development of a theoretical model of it and, consequently, perhaps toward (2) an understanding of the nature of the entire policy-making process, and also toward (3) a further explication of the concept of role as a tool for social science, in particular for political scientists in their study of political phenomena.

Therefore, this book is divided into several distinct sections: (1) a review of the work done by political scientists (judicial behavioralists); (2) a review of the work done by the major jurisprudents who have written on the subject; (3) a general discussion of the concept of role as it is usually employed in social science, and (4) a discussion of the prospects of using this concept fruitfully in the study of the appellate decision-making process with suggested types of empirical studies that might lead toward understanding that process. This last section is also highly suggestive of several operationalizations of the concept of judicial role. The fourth chapter consists of a detailed research design and a model of the appellate litigation process. The fifth chapter includes a study predicated on the design and model, as well as a report upon the findings presented, and a critique of the study with suggestions for improvements and refinements. It is hoped that the design, data, and interpretation is a sufficiently adequate initial framework and a first level of data directly relatable to any ultimate general theory of the appellate decision-making process. However, more realistically, it is assumed that the data are competent to serve as a medium by which we can demonstrate the relationship of such data to our model and various quantitative and qualitative techniques which can be used to analyze such data. Of course, I do not intend to totally abnegate the value of the findings. I simply want to qualify it appropriately.

It is difficult to resist the temptation to assist in the development of a general theory of this process. It is my desire to help produce a better ordering of the existing material and to help direct future efforts toward a comprehension of it. It seems to me that the accumulation of work done thus far in this area of the political science discipline has reached approximately the level which prompted the authors of *The American Voter* to state:

The construction of such a framework would solve several problems that have harassed empirical work in the social sciences. When a field of investigation is opened, small exploratory studies turn up isolated relationships between assorted variables in the area of inquiry. These relationships have a good deal of intrinsic interest and cast a welcome light upon some corner of the phenomenon being observed. Yet as such studies multiply the flow of unrelated findings becomes more confusing than enlightening. The conceptual tools of analysis are so varied that they defy any simple ordering by the interested reader. Increasingly, the sense of the coherent accumulation of knowledge, which the empirical approach originally seemed to hold in store is lost.

As improved methods permit a drastic expansion of hypothesis testing, pressure increases toward construction of a framework into which findings from a variety of sources may be placed. In the earliest phase of empirical effort, a concept may come into use as much because of its amenability to measurement as its relevance to the problem at hand. Theoretical contributions are small and piecemeal. But as empirical access broadens, the question becomes less what *can* be measured than what is *most strategic* to be applied: how well does it fit into a broader theoretical orientation?[2]

It is hoped that the framework which has come out of the following analysis of the relevant literature is not akin to an oversimplified explanation of patently complex phenomena against which the authors of *The American Voter* have cautioned. The writer believes that though there has been much simplification herein, the main jurisprudential theoretical variables have been accounted for. It is acknowledged that this is, hopefully, only the beginning—both in framework and in the specific nature of the universe studied in the field.

---

[2] Angus Campbell, et al., *The American Voter* (New York: John Wiley and Sons, 1960), pp. 18–19.

Chapter I

Review of the Literature:
The Political Behavioralists

POLITICAL scientists have spent a good deal of time, energy, and money in studying some of the operations and results of the United States Supreme Court process. The vast bulk of this work is most accurately characterized as legal and historical description and analysis of the product of that process, i.e., the case decisions. Also there has been a good deal of structural description of the court system. Not until lately has much been done by these scholars to increase the knowledge of the actual mechanism of the process itself and its dynamic functioning. Charles Hyneman's statement on this point is worth quoting at some length:

> The consequences of subordination of description to other purposes is readily observed in our writing about constitutional law and judicial enforcement of constitutional limitations. Our [political science] literature on this subject is voluminous. . . . The main purpose in this part of our study has not been to describe a set of relationships that endure with sufficient consistency to be called a system. Rather, the main purpose has been to make clear what meanings the judiciary has given to provisions of the United States Constitution, to show what has happened to legislation as a consequence of judicial determinations of constitutionality, and to evaluate critically the premises

and beliefs of judges and the reasoning by which they justified their decisions.[1]

Today, the notion of the Supreme Court as a positive policy-making organ is just about totally accepted in political science circles.[2] Moreover, the general political functions of courts in society have been carefully investigated by many sociologists and anthropologists through the last thirty or so years.[3]

Perhaps the major recent development in the reevaluation by political scientists of the proper scope of study of the Anglo-American adjudicatory machinery has come in the writings and views of the political behavioralists. These political scientists either borrow the theories and methods of various social sciences intact, make modifications thereon, or formulate and construct their own theory and methodology for their study of various psy-

---

[1] Charles Hyneman, *The Study of Politics* (Urbana: University of Illinois Press, 1960), p. 41.

[2] Among many others, some of the better statements can be found in David B. Truman, *The Governmental Process* (New York: Alfred A. Knopf, 1951); Victor G. Rosenblum, *Law as a Political Instrument* (New York: Doubleday, 1955); Glendon Schubert, *Constitutional Politics* (New York: Holt, Rinehart & Winston, 1960); Robert Dahl, "The Role of the Supreme Court as National Policy Maker," *Journal of Public Law*, 61 (1957), 279; Learned Hand, *The Bill of Rights* (Cambridge: Harvard University Press, 1960); Robert Jackson, "The Supreme Court as a Political Institution," reproduced in Alan F. Westin's *The Supreme Court: Views from Inside* (New York: W. W. Norton, 1961). A recent article notes also that the courts have substantial policy-making functions in the criminal area as well as those areas of law more commonly considered to be political, i.e., constitutional law, administrative law, etc.:

> It would seem obvious, therefore, that the issue is not which branch of government ought to assume responsibility for major policy decisions, but rather the issue is the relative functions which the legislature, the judiciary, and the administrative agency ought to play.

Frank J. Remington and V. G. Rosenblum, "The Criminal Law and the Legislative Process," *Law Forum* (Winter, 1960), 481–99.

[3] The list is extensive. Two relatively recent books which are excellent illustrations of this type of work are: E. Adamson Hoebel, *The Law of Primitive Man* (Cambridge: Harvard University Press, 1955); Max Gluckman, *The Judicial Process of the Barotse of Northern Rhodesia* (Manchester: Manchester University Press, 1954).

chological and sociological aspects of the political process.[4] Nevertheless, as I noted in the Introduction, that which has been done by them still leaves much to be desired.

Probably the major charges to be brought against the current group of political science's judicial behavioralists concern the use to which they put both their adopted theory and their borrowed methodology. As to the former, the principal complaints are that the judicial behavioralists, for the most part, extend theoretical social science concepts far beyond their recognizable conceptual and operational boundaries;[5] fail to show any linkage between the work done in the other social science fields and such theories and concepts; often fail to denote adequately the theoretical import to their empirical work before and after the study is conducted; and even seem not to appreciate the important subtleties of scientific work, particularly the notion of the null hypothesis in empirical testing and the traps involved in overgeneralizing from acquired data. The following pages contend that only on rare occasions can we even begin to find an implicit notion of a judicial decision-making theory to which the particular study might find relationship. Worse still, much of the work done seems to be quite irrelevant for any such theory.

---

[4] This movement is, of course, the political behavioralist movement in political science. Its content and mood are well examined in an article by Robert Dahl, "The Behavioral Approach in Political Science: Epitaph for a Monument to a Successful Protest," *American Political Science Review*, 55 (Dec., 1961), 763–72.

[5] The most recent clear-cut case of this is Professor Stuart Nagel's use of the sociological and social psychological concept "sociometric relationship." As it has been used in these disciplines, this concept refers to like and dislike relationships and interactions among people in groups. Sociometric techniques are designed to study and measure such phenomena as interpersonal relations like attractions, repulsions and indifferences. One cannot help wondering why Professor Nagel attempts to stretch its meaning to include the action of one court in formally overruling the decisions of an inferior court. Surely a decision to overrule does not mean that the judges do not like the judges of the lower court. His study would add nothing to the sociometric work done by sociologists, and his usage of the concept only clouds his purpose, whatever it may be. "Sociometric Relations Among American Courts," *Southwestern Social Science Quarterly*, 43 (Sept., 1962), 136–42.

As to methodology, the charges would run along parallel lines with those on theory. The main point is that it is not surprising, in light of the great lack of any decision-making theoretical guidelines, to find distortion in the employment of social science methods in studying the judicial decision-making process. This is due to the complementary nature of theory and method.

In order to systematically survey and analyze an area of study, one must utilize or devise a classification scheme. Since this analysis will be dealing with the theory, method, and data sources thus far employed by political science judicial behavioralists and since these three aspects of research all are intimately and inextricably intertwined, we need only select one of these aspects as our basis of categorization in order to include the material of all three. The choice is that of theory as this is my own academic orientation. Thus, the various works to be analyzed are grouped in relationship to their particular theoretical or key conceptual foundations.

Near the outset of his career, Glendon Schubert, the leading judicial behavioralist in the political science discipline, stated that he was concerned with understanding the behavior of judges.[6] Therefore, as a man well-versed in the materials of social psychology, Professor Schubert was in quest of isolating and understanding that which motivated a judge to decide one way or another. In his own words, his concern was

> . . . with the socio-psychological dimension of formal decision-making behavior of this small, political elite group. [The] primary concern is with the *motivations* which lead individual members of this small group to choose, in their conjoint voting behavior, to select (sic) certain alternatives rather than others.[7]

This is very much the same study commitment, as we shall see subsequently, which has been of great concern to many legal

---

[6] Schubert, *op. cit.;* Schubert's first major work, however, was a traditional type of study. See *The Presidency in the Courts* (Minneapolis: University of Minnesota Press, 1957). His first judicial behavior opus was *Quantitative Analysis of Judicial Behavior* (Glencoe, Illinois: The Free Press, 1959).

[7] *Quantitative Analysis* . . ., p. 11.

philosophers. But the concepts and methods that Schubert and most of the other judicial behavioralists use are radically different. Note well from the above quotation: Professor Schubert has stated that his concern is with the motivations behind the judicial decision and the psychological and sociological aspects thereof. This seems to be a fair starting point for the whole field of judicial behavior. But of course the concept of motivation is far too general and, in fact, has fallen into disrepute in the discipline of psychology as being almost operationally meaningless.[8] However, the most popular motivational concept employed is that of attitude.

JUDICIAL ATTITUDE

Schubert and Spaeth

Professors Schubert and Harold J. Spaeth are the two main employers of the social psychological concept of attitude and use it as the basic building block in their projected theory of judicial motivation. Schubert and Spaeth, through their systematic study of a myriad of case votes and opinions, have observed and measured judicial bloc behavior on many policy issues.[9] Their precise accounts of this phenomenon comprise the vast preponderance of their published work. It is fair to assume that either before, during, or after the initiation of their work in this area, these two scholars concluded (or hypothesized) that what accounted for very substantial agreement or disagreement between groups of judges on various issues was *not* a coincidence of legal reasoning ability among groups of judges which resulted in coincidence of decision between several judges and in disagreement with another group of judges. In other words, if one made the *a priori* assumption that the judicial process is verily a vehicle by which revealed truth is discovered through skill in legal logic, it would follow that palpably observable dispute be-

[8] See Charles N. Cofer's conclusion in his study on "Motivation," *Annual Review of Psychology*, 10 (1959).

[9] A complete bibliography of Schubert's and Spaeth's works can be found in the bibliographical section of Schubert's *Judicial Decision-Making* (New York: The Free Press of Glencoe, 1963).

tween large blocs of the Court could be interpreted to arise as a result of one group of judges simply having mastered the necessary legal ability while the other group has failed to master it and is grossly inferior. Few political scientists buy this line of argument, and Schubert and Spaeth are hardly the exceptions. Being versed in the advancement of social science concepts and method, Schubert and Spaeth, not surprisingly, find more satisfactory explanation in the coincidence of attitudes of the judges as that factor which is responsible for the described agreement and disagreement.

Of course one might wonder why these scholars, being so versed, totally discount the possibility that the judges' personalities (either singly or in interaction with attitudes) account for the observed bloc cohesion. Nevertheless the big question that we ask is: Can they demonstrate the fact that judicial decisions are dependent upon attitude through their methods and data?

The use of sophisticated social science methodology (e.g., Guttman Scale analysis and factor analysis) to analyze case votes and opinions in order to arrive at an understanding of the judicial process by understanding judicial motivation, i.e., attitudes, seems to have several major drawbacks. As noted, the Schubert-Spaeth type of study seems to convince many people that their basic assumption about the effect of attitude on the judicial decision is correct. *But in our view these studies do not do this and cannot do this.* They can and do simply demonstrate very precisely that such blocs exist, and they can and do clearly delineate the boundaries of such blocs. But that this bloc behavior is related to specifically relevant attitude positions of the decision-makers is still only an *a priori* assumption. Insight into this problem might be gained by a review of the literature on legislative and popular voting behavior. From the Schubert-Spaeth perspective, these areas must have much in common with the judicial process, for a vote is, after all, a vote. Yet even a quick glance at some of the legislative materials reveals that many institutional factors play significant roles in bringing about bloc cohesion. For instance, according to David B. Truman:

To discern stable patterns of behavior among the complexities of the Congressional parties is a matter of the utmost difficulty. Members of the Congress are not automatons but reasoning men and women acting in a setting in which they are subject to a bewildering barrage of conflicting, or at the least inconsistent, demands—from within their constituencies, from organized and unorganized interests both narrower and more extensive than their electoral districts, from within the Congress itself, and from their own conceptions of what is required for the strength and survival of the polity of which they are among the most important trustees. *The actions of these men and women are not to be accounted for by any simple ascription of motive or intent, and this injunction applies with special force when these actions are manifest primarily in the form of a series of record votes.*[10]

Moreover, the problem and inadequacies of measuring that which is considered to be an intervening psychological variable influencing a vote (in this case, attitude) by going to the vote itself is stated most excellently in *The American Voter:*

The importance of stable partisan loyalties has been universally recognized in electoral studies, but the manner in which they should be defined and measured has been a subject of some disagreement. In keeping with the conception of party identification as a psychological tie, these orientations have been measured in our research by asking individuals to describe their own partisan loyalties. Some studies, however, have chosen to *measure stable partisan orientation in terms of an individual's past voting record* or in terms of his attitude on a set of partisan issues. Thus Republican and Democratic identification are sometimes defined as those who vote consistently for the same party and "Independents" as those who do not. The fact that a definition of this sort serves many practical and scholarly purposes underscores the immense influence of party identification in motivating behavior. *But we feel that such a definition blurs the distinction between the psychological state and its behavioral consequences.* We have not measured party attachments in terms of the vote or the evaluation of partisan issues because we are

---

[10] David B. Truman, *The Congressional Party* (New York: John Wiley and Sons, 1959), p. 279 (emphasis added).

interested in exploring the influence of party identification on voting behavior and its immediate determinants. *When an independent measure of party identification is used it is clear that even strong party adherents at times may think and act in contradiction to their party allegiance. We could never establish the conditions under which this will occur if lasting party orientations are measured in terms of the behavior they are thought to affect.*[11]

The writer believes that Schubert and Spaeth have not met this problem adequately.

Another apparent misuse by Professor Schubert of the data of judicial votes and opinions in relationship to psychological explanatory concepts (including and in addition to attitude) is found in two of his later works.[12] In Hullian fashion, he sets up the stimulus-response bond scheme with the case (the facts within the judicial opinion itself) as the stimulus (S) and the vote (the decision of the court) as the response (R). The former is the independent variable and the latter, of course, the dependent variable. The intervening variable is the judge himself, or his attitude or attitude universe. The conceptual difficulty in this scheme is that these facts, as gleaned from the opinion verbiage, are not a stimulus at all. Are the facts as they are stated in the judicial opinion the same facts presented to the court for decision? No, they are not. The case opinion itself was not that which confronted the perceiving organisms (the judges) at the argument. That set of facts (presented in the opinion) was not the same which, after perception, filtered through the attitude net (behavioral predisposition set) and triggered the response. The case opinion itself represents a *distillation* of the stimulus, which was the actual factual situation presented to the court. Hasn't Professor Schubert utilized the response itself as a stimulus? So it seems.

If Schubert is going to employ factor analysis techniques to

---

[11] Campbell, et al., *op. cit.*, p. 122 (emphasis added).

[12] Glendon Schubert, "A Psychometric Model of the Supreme Court," *American Behavioral Scientist,* 5 (Nov., 1961), 14–18; and "The 1960 Term of the Supreme Court: A Psychometric Analysis," *American Political Science Review,* 56 (March, 1962), 90–107.

present a set of actual factors (stimuli) that relate to an ultimate decision which is an output from a psychological process of decision-makers, then he must go to the *actual fact sources* themselves in order to maximize the potential validity of his findings. He should go to the briefs before the court, get a verbatim record of the oral argument, obtain copies of the clerks' memos, obtain a record of what was said at the conference, etc. Of course there are varying degrees of near-impossibility of access to the latter three, but this issue must be faced squarely. After-the-fact facts are not the real thing.

Thus Schubert has tried to explain behavior by that behavior itself because he is trying too hard to apply theoretical schemes and concepts from other branches of the social sciences that just will not work with his selected data source. His choice of phenomena to study just seems to cause no end of trouble for the concept of attitude and its related theoretical structures.

A frequently iterated and reiterated charge against some of the work by these behavioralists is that great emphasis is placed upon heavy quantification for the purpose of quantification only. One source of this charge can be traced to the problems involved in trying to link everything to attitude. An example of this point can be observed in Schubert's discussion of "judicial superannuation."[13] Much effort, to be sure, was spent in collecting the detailed quantitative information on the average ages of justices at their death or upon their retirement and the average age of the justices over the decades. These data are presented as substantiation of his claim that Supreme Court justices, particularly in the 1930s, tend to be "very old." There is an inference, not to be ignored, that there may well be a relationship between a judge's age and both the soundness of his reasoning and the modernity of his value-attitude system. But "very old" means very little. Obviously this data is not in the least sufficient to support implicit theories on the connection between advanced

---

[13] *Constitutional Politics*, pp. 57–66. Though not explicity defined by Schubert, the concept of judicial superannuation is probably best conceptualized as "Several very old men are in very important governmental positions."

age and either incompetence or physiologically based conservatism. The fact that during the middle thirties the average ages of justices was in the mid-sixties and that it is currently under-sixty years of age proves nothing but those facts alone. Once again the emphasis for explanation centers on attitude. Once again we are left with the vaguest inference, and inference is scarcely solid proof.

In bringing this type of research up to date one finds little change in the conceptual orientation and the claims made for the work done. Professor Schubert has restated in three recent works the importance of scaling attitudes through *judicial votes* in order to explain judicial behavior.[14] In reading through his material one does occasionally find an allusion to the less-than-probative nature of this work. For instance, in his substantive contribution to his 1963 reader he stated that

> A Supreme Court justice is an individual, and a case before the Court for decision can be conceptualized as asking the justice to respond by his vote on the merits, signifying his attitude toward the major value or values at stake in the decision. Certainly it is not prima facie unreasonable to suggest that the seven recent cases dealing with judicial review of courts martial jurisdiction were testing the individual attitudes of the justices toward a basic value in our constitutional system: civil supremacy over the military. . . .[15]

However it is a far cry from this mild suggestion, which is of course justifiable as a hypothesis to be tested, to his forceful statement (made upon another review of the accumulation of much similarly collected and similarly interpreted data) that the judicial behavioralists, among others, "have *debunked* legal prin-

---

[14] "Civilian Control and *Stare Decisis* in the Warren Court," and "From Public Law to Judicial Behavior," in *Judicial Decision-Making;* "Judicial Attitudes and Voting Behavior: The 1961 Term of the United States Supreme Court," *Law and Contemporary Problems,* 28 (Winter, 1963), 100–142; "Bibliographical Essay: Behavioral Research in Public Law," *American Political Science Review,* 57 (June, 1963), 433–45.

[15] "Civilian Control . . .," p. 58.

ciples as factors controlling decisions."[16] Yet, strangely enough, Schubert discovers in the reader article discussed above that

> An examination of Clark's opinions reveals a perfectly clear and unambiguous reliance upon yet another new independent variable: the time honored common-law principle of *stare decisis*.[17]

Now it is not important to stress this inconsistency for its own sake. It is mentioned for two purposes: First, it points out the difficulties that Schubert himself is having in reconciling his own theory with the facts; Second, it may augur, at last, a change in the perspective underlying his assumptions. This, it is submitted, must lead to a change in his methodological orientation. However, although this work *is* a departure in thought from his own and his followers' works, it has several flaws in it which are mentioned in subsequent discussion.

Professor Spaeth, in his contribution to Schubert's *Judicial Decision-Making*, manifests a bit of the same type of a scientific immodesty which characterizes much of Schubert's work. In the conclusion to his study which found that "Judicial choice in these cases continued to hinge upon the justices' attitudes toward business" Spaeth states that

> If, as seems likely, further application of psychometric techniques of analysis should demonstrate that the Court does render virtually all its decisions on the basis of the operation of a very few basic attitudes, extensive reinterpretation may be required of the standard explanations of Supreme Court decision-making.[18]

The foundation for this misunderstanding of the nature of the data they have obtained seems to lie at least partially in a misconception of the nature of hypothesis testing in social (or any) science. Both Schubert and Spaeth (as well as some other members of the political science judicial behavior movement) appear to be guilty of not comprehending the general function of the null hypothesis in testing and how this relates to problems

---

[16] "Judicial Attitudes . . .," p. 104 (emphasis added).
[17] "Civilian Control . . .," p. 71.
[18] "Warren Court Attitudes towards Business: The B. Scale," in *Judicial Decision-Making*, pp. 100–101.

of induction as stated by, among many others, Hume and Popper ("falsification"). The following is an illustration of this.

Schubert, in another of his most recent works, again attempts to prove his and Spaeth's principal hypothesis that attitudes are responsible for judicial decisional patterns. Through his Guttman scaling method and his factor analysis, Schubert believes he can test the relationship of two separate variables—the attitudes of the judges and the pattern of their decisions. If a relationship is found between the two sets of data he develops through these methods, then he believes that he has confirmed his hypothesis. But this is not so.

At best, all Schubert has done is to very precisely *describe in two ways* the composition of voting blocs. This is a valuable exercise, to be sure, but it does not at all do what it purports to do. Even if it did describe the relationship which he says it has, it would simply be a description of a possible relationship. Other plausible, rival hypotheses remain conspicuously untested. The only way they can be adequately tested is to establish a study (or studies) which will subject them to disconfirmation. The other rival hypotheses must be developed and, after operations are established, tested to see if any significant differences in behavior are produced by the action of these other hypothesized variables. If no such differences are discovered, and if these findings are verified, then, *and only then,* can we *venture* the suggestion that only one possible relationship, i.e., attitudes to decision, does not seem to be disconfirmable. However, it would seem unwise to venture this opinion upon the type of inferences made from such descriptive work posited by Schubert, Spaeth, and others.

Campbell and Stanley attempt to explain why scientists find this notion so hard to swallow and further elaborate on this idea of proof and disconfirmation:

> The notion that experiments never "confirm" theory, while correct, goes so against our attitudes and experiences as scientists as to be almost intolerable. Particularly does this emphasis seem unsatisfactory vis-a-vis the elegant and striking confirmations encountered in physics and chemistry, where the experimental

data may fit in minute detail over numerous points of measurement a complex curve predicted by the theory. And the perspective becomes phenomenologically unacceptable to most of us when extended to the inductive achievements of vision. For example, it is hard to realize that the tables and chairs which we "see" before us are not "confirmed" or "proven" by the visual evidence, but are merely hypotheses about external objects not as yet disconfirmed by the multiple probes of the visual system. There is a grain of truth in these reluctances. Varying degrees of "confirmation" are conferred upon a theory through the number of *plausible rival hypotheses* available to account for the data. The fewer such plausible rival hypotheses remaining, the greater the degree of "confirmation." Presumably at any stage of accumulation of evidence, even for the most advanced science, there are numerous possible theories compatible with the data, particularly if all theories involving complex contingencies be allowed. Yet, for "well established" theories, and theories thoroughly probed by complex experiments, few if any rivals may be practically available or seriously proposed. This fewness is the epistemological counterpart of the positive affirmation of theory which elegant experiments seem to offer.[19]

The major methodological objection to the work dealing in attitudes using these statistical techniques has come from Joel Grossman.[20] Professor Grossman was apparently motivated to criticize the relationship of scalogram analysis and the inferences drawn from the results by some peculiar interpretations derived from the data in several of the studies. One of these by Professor S. Sidney Ulmer was that, according to a consistent interpretation of the scalogram data, Felix Frankfurter is conceived of as having unsympathetic attitudes toward civil liberties.[21] This distressed Grossman.

---

[19] Donald T. Campbell and Julian Stanley, "Experimental and Quasi-Experimental Designs for Research on Teaching," in N. L. Gage (ed.), *Handbook of Research on Teaching* (Chicago: Rand McNally, 1963), pp. 205–6.

[20] Joel B. Grossman, "Role Playing and the Analysis of Judicial Behavior: The Case of Mr. Justice Frankfurter," *Journal of Public Law,* 11 (1962), 285–309.

[21] See "Analysis of Behavior Patterns on the United States Supreme Court," *Journal of Politics,* 22 (Nov., 1960), 653.

Grossman pointed to several deficiencies in the method which allowed for what he considered to be a great distortion of reality, i.e., of this part of Frankfurter's attitude universe. Ulmer's conclusion about Frankfurter *is* consistent with the objective data revealed in the study and with the theory of Guttman scaling. But, according to Grossman,

> The questionable procedure lies in the recruitment of data to be processed. What has been done is that a "category" of cases constructed on one factor common to all cases in that category also determines the responses of the Justices to the extent that it "limits" their choices "requiring" a Justice to cast his vote either for or against *that* factor. This factor is chosen arbitrarily —as it must be. But the very arbitrariness of the decision itself becomes a factor to be accounted for in determining the conclusion.
>
> Here, the arbitrary factor is the category which encompasses certain species of cases. We must realize that these categories may conceivably be tools of academic analysis which have been used for the convenience of interpreters of constitutional law. They may not be the same categories into which the Justices themselves divide the cases they are to decide. Whatever the usefulness of such classifications, it is not a comprehensive but a limited utility. In light of the knowledge which we now possess, it is hardly shocking to suggest that a single case would be approached differently by individual judges. For example, it is quite conceivable that a case involving a double jeopardy claim, i.e., *Bartkus v. Illinois,* would be viewed by Mr. Justice Douglas as a civil liberties deprivation . . . by Mr. Justice Frankfurter as primarily a question of achieving a federal balance in criminal proceedings . . . and by Mr. Justice Clark as a question of efficacy of certain types of law enforcement procedure. Clearly each of the Justices mentioned viewed the consequences of the decision differently because to each it poses a different problem. Each Justice is, in effect, responding to a different variable. . . . How accurate is it, therefore, to record all of the Justices as having voted for *or* against a civil liberties claim. . . ?[22]

This is an excellent statement of the problem. Grossman goes on to note that, in his view, the real problem thus far resides

---

[22] Grossman, *op. cit.,* p. 293.

in the fact that the scalogram analysts of judicial behavior have confined their data so stringently and extracted their "working data so very sparsely from the wealth available" that they have said, in effect, "very little." However, he believes that scalogram analysis can indeed be put to better use.

According to Grossman there are obviously factors other than attitudes which play a part in the judicial process. In passing, he lists them quite generally as structural, institutional, psychological and philosophical factors. Specifically he notes that one main factor other than substantive attitude is surely relevant in the particular case of his interest (Frankfurter), namely, Frankfurter's concept of role. He then defines this role (as a factor involved in deciding cases) as the denial of judicial responsibility (DJR). His hypothesis was that Frankfurter was the justice most responsive to this factor. Judicial responsibility as an element or factor includes questions of jurisdiction, federalism, and deference to other governmental units. Moreover, this factor must have been mentioned in the cases—and was frequently mentioned by Frankfurter himself. Of course it is not surprising that Frankfurter was most responsive, and that many of the times he so responded the substantive issue was in the civil rights field of law.

Grossman himself, however, recognized the limitations of even this extension of the scalogram technique. He stated that the DJR factor is a rare one and would be difficult to discover in many situations. For instance:

> There is no evidence that the DJR factor would enable us to gain insights into, say, Mr. Justice Stewart's responses. . . .[23]

In his eyes, the saving grace in his use of the scalogram is that he has used it as a *corrective* device for the other scalogram analyses which are incapable of explaining much nuance in judicial behavior, e.g., Frankfurter's explicit and oft-stated concept of the function of the justice.

Though I am in accord with Professor Grossman's criticism

---

[23] *Ibid.*, p. 308.

of the scalogram and what it can do, I feel much less sanguine about the helpfulness of the innovation. After all, can the scalogram really help us in analyzing the role of the judicial decision-maker? Grossman would have us believe so. However, a careful look at what is being done here discloses otherwise. All that has been accomplished in this study is the isolation and analysis of just another *attitude*.[24] This is essentially the same problem in Schubert's discovery and handling of *stare decisis* discussed above. In this case it is Frankfurter's attitude toward judicial functions of the Supreme Court of the United States as a branch of the tripartite system of American government. Grossman has not, as he has claimed, studied another of the factors which in interaction produces (in his own words) "a fathomable and concrete result—a decision in a particular case. . . ." We have simply seen scalogram analysis operating on another attitude which is at substantially the same level as the particular substantive area of law attitudes assumedly germane to the cases.

The possible judicial role factors which may be important to isolate, observe, and measure (so it seems to me) are at a deeper and more integrated psychic level and are probably not at all subject to scalogram scrutiny. Nonetheless, Grossman's critique of the method is quite helpful.

To date there are only two studies of the judicial process which *directly* (as being distinct from the justices' statement of the law) isolate and measure the attitudes of judges. One is by Stuart Nagel. Nagel stated that

Since 1959, at least three articles and one book have been published with titles indicating that they deal with the attitudes of some segment of the American judiciary. However, these studies are concerned only with the on-the-bench attitudes of judges as manifested in judicial decisions. As yet no study seems

---

[24] This same argument holds for Spaeth's notion of judicial power. After all, this restraint of the judge is simply, as he admits, defined in political, rather than in legal, terms. The judge has simply allowed one political attitude to prevail over another. "Judicial Power as a Variable Motivating Supreme Court Behavior," *Midwest Journal of Political Science*, 6 (May, 1962), 54–82.

to have been made of the more general attitudes of the American judiciary.[25]

In order to learn the judges' attitudes, he employed the questionnaire technique. In a great departure from the normal political science methodology in this area, Nagel pointedly asked the judges what their attitudes on many areas were. Then each questionnaire was scored and each judge placed, according to his answers, somewhere on a liberalism-conservatism scale. From this point, it was simple enough to test whether or not there was any correlation between their personal attitudes and their decisions while on the bench. Nagel found a moderate to slight correlation between a conservative score and a judge's votes for the prosecution in criminal cases, for the defendant in business regulation cases, for the defendant in automobile accident cases, and for the employer in employee injury cases. He then went on to state that there was no relationship between those situations where the judges apparently voted against their attitudes and the fact that the judge did or did not wear a robe when deciding cases; did or did not have longer judicial experience; and was or was not considered a legal scholar. This is an important study even though it has failed to account for any variables which are significantly related to decisions which are apparently contrary to their decisional predispositions.

There are, however, two main caveats to attach to the conclusion that "conservative off-the-bench attitudes seemed to be reflected in the decisions reached by these jurists." First, the sample analyzed is hardly a representative one. After all, out of 313 judges contacted, only 119 answered Nagel's questionnaire. Thus the barely significant statistical results are called into question as to becoming even part of the empirical base for any generalization about the judicial decision-making process. This 35 per cent of the judiciary are in this sense a rare breed. Second, there is a serious problem involved in measuring the attitudes of judges through the use of the questionnaire employed

---

[25] "Off-the-Bench Attitudes," in Judicial Decision-Making, p. 29.

by Nagel. It would appear that the broader the attitude universe demarcated by the attitude-evoking device, the less singular influence it might have upon the particular observed action. Too many other factors, e.g., other attitude universes, role, etc., may well impinge into the matrix of factors responsible for behavior. Nevertheless, Nagel's work in this area is a significant step forward.

The other such study is a very recent one by David J. Danelski of Yale University.[26] Actually, Danelski prefers to discuss the value systems rather than the attitude systems of the justices. However, at this point in the development of political science and particularly in this branch of it, these two concepts can be thought of as being (by-and-large) interchangeable.

Danelski's piece is the most sophisticated and modest of its content type. Its purpose is to advance us toward a theory—and it does do that. More specifically, Danelski tries to isolate and gauge the predisposition of the judge independent of the case opinions of that judge, and then show us the statistical relationship of this value position to the judge's own opinions and voting behavior. This is as Nagel did. Instead of going to the judges personally, however (and running the risk of a potentially minimal validity), Danelski uses Ralph K. White's value analysis technique[27] on some off-the-bench *public addresses* of the judges. In addition to this methodological innovation, Danelski is the first to substantially grapple with various other attitudinal variants directly related to behavior, i.e., the intensity to which the attitude or value is held, and the congruency and cognitive completeness of the values. Thus Danelski has attempted, most wisely, to develop a discrete value variable with which to work. All of this is clearly an advance over the work of the Schubert school.

Danelski's attempt at verification of the value-decision hypotheses is through Schubert-type scaling and factor analysis.

---

[26] David J. Danelski, "Values as Variables in Judicial Decision-Making: Notes Toward a Theory." Paper delivered at the 1964 Midwest Conference of Political Scientists, Madison, Wisconsin.

[27] Ralph K. White, *Value Analysis* (Glen Gardner, New Jersey: Society for the Study of Social Issues, 1953).

He reports some success in this. The main difference between Danelski's procedure and Schubert's is that Danelski has used the statistical technique meaningfully for explanation. He himself observes this:

> This paper has demonstrated the utility of factor analysis and cumulative scaling in the study of judicial behavior. In the past these techniques have been used, for the most part, to describe judicial behavior precisely. Here they were used for purposes of verification of hypotheses.[28]

But most important is the stated recognition that there are many other factors which must be taken into account in developing a theory of judicial decision-making. Unfortunately, Danelski goes no further in even conceptually setting forth what these other factors might be or how they might interact.

On the whole though, it seems to this writer that overzealousness in borrowing one of the most widely used and explanatorily powerful social science concepts (attitude) and an overemphasis on the *explanatory* utility of statistical techniques had led several political science judicial behavioralists into a difficult position. Had they been content to stress the importance of the precision inherent in their *description* they would be standing on reasonably safe ground. However, their insistence on discussing their explanation of the judicial process through highly questionable applications of the concept of attitude and some related conceptual schemes, plus less-than-neat generalization from the data, have left them open to occasionally reckless charges and to much apathy from legal and other social science circles. But despite this negative reception, they persist in their undertaking and their work still dominates the field.[29] This is an unfortunate state of affairs. But it is not unique. There is further trouble of

---

[28] Danelski, "Values as Variables . . .," p. 23, note 26.

[29] See Harold J. Spaeth, "Unidimensionality and Item Variance in Judicial Scaling." Paper delivered at the 1964 Convention of the American Political Science Association, Chicago, Illinois. Stuart Nagel's most recent effort puts a heavy emphasis on prediction through statistics. See "Applying Correlation Analysis to Case Prediction," *Texas Law Review*, 42 (Oct., 1964), 1006–17.

this same sort in the utilization of the concepts of small-group dynamics theory in the study of the judicial decision-making process.

SMALL GROUP THEORY

Ulmer, Snyder, and Danelski

Professor S. Sidney Ulmer, who is closely identified with the Schubert movement, has generally been considered to be the leading group theory[30] practitioner among students of the Supreme Court of the United States as well as of the judicial process in general. In a recent essay he offered several reasons why he believes it to be difficult to study the Court from this perspective:

> One who would study leadership on a collegial court faces, at the outset, what are clearly substantial obstacles. The "purple curtain" that hides much of the doings of courts of law is no accident. By design, great care is taken to safeguard deliberations leading to decision, and the conference room of the collegial court especially is considered inviolate. Such practices are neither arbitrary nor superfluous, since an important function of obscuring decisional processes is to sustain the myth of judicial objectivity which permeates the American judicial system.[31]

Ulmer, like Schubert, appears eager to refute the "myth" of judicial objectivity and to ridicule the secrecy cloaking judicial conference proceedings. He does, however, recognize and stress the limitations that this procedure does place upon the use of group theory to explain this decision-making process:

---

[30] Group theory, in the David B. Truman sense of interest, is probably best applied to the courts in the work of E. Clement Vose and Frank Sorauf. See Vose's "Litigation as a Form of Pressure Group Activity," *Annals of the American Academy of Political and Social Science*, 319 (1958), 20–31; and Sorauf's "*Zorach v. Clauson:* The Impact of a Supreme Court Decision," *American Political Science Review*, 53 (Sept., 1959), 777–91.

[31] "Leadership in the Michigan Supreme Court," in *Judicial Decision-Making*, pp. 13–14.

> Thus it cannot be emphasized too much that the type of em-
> pirical material available on collegial courts is, in the last
> analysis, a rather crude indicator of what we seek—influence
> structure of the group.[32]

I agree heartily but want to specify the reasons for my concur-
rence and also to point out that which Ulmer has apparently
neglected to mention. It might be added that my objections here
are very much akin to those concerning the work of Professors
Schubert and Spaeth. This is so because Ulmer deals with substantially the same methodology and substantially the same data.
Only the concepts and theoretical schemata have been changed.
Even the basic assumptions have not been altered by Professor
Ulmer. A rose by any other name. . . . But let me be more
concrete.

Ulmer commences each of his small group theory essays with
an interesting general statement about small group theory. He
painstakingly discusses the concepts of small groups, leadership,
influence, and interaction. He continues by discussing some of
the generally accepted tenets such as: all groups have leaders;
leaders influence their members; this leader influence is observable and measurable. Further elaboration of this last point includes the notion that one way in which influence is measured
is through ratios of supportive–nonsupportive behavior received
and given by group members. This, of course, is where and how
Ulmer once again brings us to the judicial vote and opinion. In
essence, judicial blocs are now labelled as inter-individual soli-
darity. Whereas the small group theorists ordinarily discuss the
notion of attraction of one member to another as an influence
factor, and usually refer to the physical or emotional type of
attraction, Ulmer is interested in the attraction power of each
judge's attitudes and values for every other judge. This assumption has a familiar ring to it. Of course small group theorists do
speak of attitude attraction—it is just that we want to note that
we have returned to a familiar conceptual ground.

The fact that Professor Ulmer states that he is using small

---

[32] *Ibid.*, p. 15.

group theory and methodology does not alter the fact that he is not. In adopting the group theory conceptual scheme, he cites Robert Bales's work as authority. But it is widely known that Bales's behavioral units of observation and analysis are the products of laboratory groups which have had their every action (physical and verbal) carefully scrutinized by highly trained observers. Bales's concepts and techniques relate to group *dynamics* and trace interaction over time. Why Ulmer chooses these concepts to cover his bloc analysis is somewhat of a mystery. Ulmer has not analyzed dynamic behavior. He has simply retreated, as do Professors Schubert and Spaeth, into the law books to count votes.

It is proper to re-emphasize that Ulmer himself notes several weaknesses to his own study and states that he simply hopes that it has been explorative and suggestive. My point is that it is simply, no more and no less, a bloc analysis. The use of small group dynamics theory concepts adds little to nothing. A similar critique can be made of the work of sociologist (turned political behavioralist), Eloise Snyder, whose judicial behavioral study

> deals with the Supreme Court as a small group and attempts to discover what group processes are present as the Justices solve the important problems brought before them.[33]

It would be quite worthwhile to test some aspects of current group theory against relevant data concerning the Supreme Court. However, all we find in Professor Snyder's work is still another bloc analysis. For instance, we are informed that justices tend to "clique off" and that certain judges are pivotal on each Court.

There is nothing in this study of a group of nine men that couldn't be and hasn't been done with either 435 men or 100 men that comprise the United States House of Representatives and the Senate. And the House of Representatives, even by stretch of the "sociological imagination," is not a small group.

---

[33] Eloise Snyder, "The Supreme Court as a Small Group," *Social Forces*, 36 (March, 1958), 232–38.

The *one* study published to date which *is* based upon group dynamics theory and which has done more than make inferences from voting behavior is another research endeavor by Danelski. In this study, he systematically attempted to study the conference leadership role, opinion assignment role, and group unification role of the Chief Justice of the United States Supreme Court.[34] Essentially, Professor Danelski was interested in testing the hypothesis that "the activity of the Chief Justice can be very significant in the judicial process."

The major difference between his and the other studies just reviewed is that Danelski's data related to the actual interaction between the Chief Justice and the several associates. Naturally there was no observation of the Court(s) in actual conference interaction. Instead, Danelski turned to a reasonable substitute: verbal reports. Through essays, books and letters of the justices themselves, the several chief justices, their many professional associates, and the Supreme Court clerks, conference portraits of the Taft, Hughes and Stone courts emerged.

Danelski found that because of the ability or inability of the Chief Justice to assume either "task leadership" or "social leadership" of the conference: (1) the Taft Court had conflict (though "friendly"), good cohesion, considerable satisfaction, and fair production; (2) the Hughes Court had conflict (though "bridled by the Chief"), fair cohesion, mixed satisfaction, and good production; and (3) the Stone Court had considerable conflict, poor cohesion, least satisfaction, and poor production. This condition existed in Stone's Court because, in Danelski's view, the Chief Justice could not (or did not) assume either the task leadership or social leadership of the Court in conference. Similarly, the Chief Justice's view of whether or not to try to be a "unifier" (one who discouraged dissenting opinions) is believed to have had an effect upon the Court's process and product.

Danelski is on a potentially fruitful path towards establishing

---

[34] David J. Danelski, "The Influence of the Chief Justice in the Decisional Process," in Walter F. Murphy and C. Herman Pritchett (eds.), *Courts, Judges and Politics* (New York: Random House, 1961), pp. 497–508.

some very provocative hypotheses about the Court as a group and the impact of group-interaction and leadership variables upon the ultimate outcome of the judicial process, that is, the judicial decision. There are two major difficulties to be found in his work, however. First, it will be noted that this approach is quite highly impressionistic; though somewhat systematic, it lacks the rigor necessary for any ultimate confirmation of his hypotheses. In other words, no operations were established and no quantitative analysis offered, as in his values study. Second, one finds a disturbing lack of consistency in Danelski's system. For instance, he states that he is attempting to follow a path to an understanding of judicial behavior. Surely we can assume that *all* judicial behavior *is not significant* or of interest to us as political scientists. Strongly implied in all judicial behavioral research is the fact that we want to understand the outcome of the process. Yet, in establishing his relational scheme, Danelski has left us with what would seem to be a reasonably insignificant behavioral outcome in his study of task and social roles. In other words, we are interested in the types and degrees of conflict, cohesion, and satisfaction on any court insofar as it influences or determines the judicial decision. However, Danelski, in relating these variables (conflict, etc.) to production, operationalizes that dependent variable as the *number of conferences per week*. This, it seems, is of no greater significance for any potential theory than are the other three variables. The system of interrelationship breaks down at the crucial point, that is, at the point of establishing the key hypotheses. Yet, the study's heuristic (explorative and suggestive) importance cannot be underestimated and the approach's freshness gives hope that political science may be at the threshold of properly employing small group dynamics concepts and methodology. Moreover, it is refreshing to witness a political scientist judicial behavioralist hypothesize instead of making broad jumps to unwarranted general truths.

Group dynamics theory and its vast range of workable methodology is indeed usable by political scientists. Sociologists themselves have seen the intimate relationship between the small group and critical political concepts, e.g., democracy, and added much through their research to the store of political data and theory.[35] However, the political scientist must take care in his borrowing. It is not helpful to him or the lending discipline if the concepts are operationally distorted after the borrowing so as to be unrecognizable. It would make as little sense to borrow a concept and stipulate a conceptual definition far beyond its lexical confines.

The Supreme Court of the United States, as any appellate court, is a group. It is a small group. However, it is a most unusual group and the propositions of group dynamics do not necessarily apply. We will surely never know whether they apply unless we develop some hypotheses and test them systematically and rigorously. Danelski is the only one to have accomplished the former, in relation to courts—no one has done the latter. We surely will not know those propositions apply by reasoning or by inferring many group properties simply from voting behavior. Certainly we will add nothing to the sociologists' and social psychologists' knowledge of group dynamics by these scaling methods. Cartwright and Zander point out clearly that the three major techniques of observing patterns of interaction in the small group are: (1) experiments on individual behavior in groups (laboratory study); (2) controlled observation of social interaction (field observation); and (3) sociometric methodology.[36] Ulmer has not come close to observing his group, the Court. The fact that it is a group does not alter the fact that he has simply run a factor analysis and again disclosed bloc behavior. Only Danelski has started on the long hard road.

SOCIAL BACKGROUND ANALYSIS

Schmidhauser and Nagel

Like bloc analysis, the social background analysis is another frequently employed approach to the study of the legislative

---

[35] See Ralph K. White and Ronald Lippitt, *Autocracy and Democracy* (New York: Harper and Brothers, 1960); Sidney Verba, *Small Groups and Political Behavior* (Princeton: Princeton University Press, 1960).

[36] Dorwin Cartwright and Alvin Zander (eds.), *Group Dynamics: Research and Theory* (Evanston: Row, Peterson Company, 1960).

process which has been borrowed to assist in the behavioral study of the appellate adjudicatory process.[37] John Schmidhauser has led the political science discipline in collecting data on the social backgrounds of Supreme Court justices toward a purported objective of formulating some theory about the relationship of such a factor to judicial decisions.[38] Unfortunately, the conclusions he has reached are as difficult to interpret as some of the earlier similar types of studies of the legislative arena.

Many students of the courts (including Schmidhauser himself) feel compelled to inquire whether we need an elaborate study with charts and other mathematical accoutrement to inform us that "Educational opportunity emerges as a crucial ingredient in judicial recruitment. Every member of the Supreme Court was the recipient of law training. . . ."[39] Furthermore, at the end of the same essay we are told that "The influence of family background, while less tangible in certain respects, may be considered of great importance." The qualifying clause seems to qualify Professor Schmidhauser right out of the realm of quantification. One cannot help pondering the worth of the many charts and tables presented. Drew Pearson, although admired in certain circles for his capacities for prognostication, has never claimed scientific method as the secret behind his success. However, Pearson and Robert S. Allen stated in 1936 (after observing the personal histories of the Supreme Court justices): "In

---

[37] Two pioneers in the accumulation and analysis of social background data of legislators are Professors Charles Hyneman and Donald R. Matthews. Hyneman's work includes: "Legislative Experience of Illinois Lawmakers," *Chicago Law Review*, 3 (1935), 104, to "Who Makes Our Laws?" *Political Science Quarterly*, 55 (Dec., 1940), 556–81. Matthews is best known for two books on this topic: *The Social Background of Political Decision Makers* (Garden City, New York: Doubleday, 1954) and *U.S. Senators and Their World* (Chapel Hill: University of North Carolina Press, 1960).

[38] John R. Schmidhauser, "The Justices of the Supreme Court: A Collective Portrait," *Midwest Journal of Political Science*, 3 (Feb., 1959), 1–57; *The Supreme Court* (New York: Holt, Rinehart & Winston, 1960); with David Gold, "Scaling Supreme Court Decisions in Relation to Social Background," *PROD*, 1 (May, 1958), 6–7.

[39] The Justices of the Supreme Court . . .," p. 45.

one stroke, five corporation lawyers, their average age sixty-seven had . . . undone the work of decades. . . . Luck, plus corporation backgrounds, not constitutionality, had done its work."[40] The question, How does the simple social-background quantification *per se* advance us further than this? has not yet had, and might not have, an adequate reply.

Actually, in drawing the relationships between the accumulated data and its significance, Schmidhauser initially reverted to his major information source material, the judicial biography. For it is in the biographies that the relationship between motivational factors and correlates, e.g., personality and social background, were linked with the decision-making predisposition of a justice. Recently however, Schmidhauser and Stuart Nagel have published several articles which make some interesting observations germane to this topic. It is in this type of work that we can begin to see the possible values in social-background quantifications.

Nagel notes that although much empirical work has been done in accumulating data either upon judicial backgrounds (in the style of Schmidhauser) or upon judicial (court or individual judge) "decisional propensities" (as with Schubert, and others), no work was done in connecting these two variables theoretically through some statistical methodology and then testing various logically derivable hypotheses.[41] He then plunges onward in an effort to find the degree of correlation between certain specified background characteristics of judges (e.g., political party identi-

---

[40] *The Nine Old Men* (New York: Doubleday, Doran and Company, 1936), p. 317. Note the Schubert-like inference in the title.

[41] Social psychologists and sociologists who have worked with social background variables have *made it an inviolable practice to relate it with some other variable.* A few examples of this in relationship to political areas are: R. E. Eckert and H. C. Mills, "International Attitudes and Related Academic and Social Factors," *Journal of Educational Sociology,* 9 (1935), 142–53; P. J. Fay and W. C. Middleton, "Certain Factors Related to Liberal and Conservative Attitudes of College Students: III. Parental Membership in Certain Organizations," *Journal of Social Psychology,* 12 (1944), 55–69; Grace Rubin-Rabson, "Several Correlates of a Conservatism-Liberalism Attitude Scale," *Journal of Social Psychology,* 39 (1954), 47–55. The list is very long.

fication), and decisional tendencies (e.g., for or against the defendant in criminal actions, for or against labor in arbitration cases, for or against the defendant in automobile negligence cases, for or against the lessor in landlord-tenant cases, etc.). An illustration of his findings reveal, in this study, that the Democratic judges were more likely to hold for the defense in criminal actions than Republican judges. Carrying this study further, a more recent Nagel article has linked a judge's ethnic background to several decisional predispositions.[42] As Nagel states:

> The findings also tend to show that judges who are white Anglo-Saxon Protestants (or at·least Anglo-Saxon Protestants) tend to be found on the conservative side of split decisions on their respective courts more so than do non-Anglo-Saxon non-Protestants (or at least non-Anglo-Saxon Catholics). This finding is consistent with decision-making studies which have been made of voters and legislators. (Campbell, Gurin and Miller, *The Voter Decides*). It reflects the factors mentioned earlier which relate to economics (occupation and class), sociology (the social inheritance of values), psychology (identification with constituents and reaction to discrimination), and geography (urbanism).[43]

Schmidhauser has also recently added two articles to this type of literature. In the first of these he discovered that instead of the relationship between sectional background and the stand on the slavery issue which one would hypothesize to appear, the only split on slavery which became apparent through his objective, systematic, and quantified observations related to the justice's party affiliation (Whig or Jacksonian Democrat).[44] His

---

[42] Stuart Nagel, "Political Party Affiliation and Judge's Decisions," *American Political Science Review*, 55 (December, 1961), 843–50; see also his "Political Parties and Judicial Review in American History," *Journal of Public Law*, 11 (1962), 328–40; "Ethnic Affiliation and Judicial Propensities," *Journal of Politics*, 24 (1962), 92–110; and "Testing Relations between Judicial Characteristics and Judicial Decision-Making," *Western Political Quarterly*, 15 (Sept., 1962), 425–37.

[43] "Ethnic Affiliation . . .," pp. 109–10.

[44] "Judicial Behavior and the Sectional Crisis of 1837–1860," *Journal of Politics*, 23 (Nov., 1961), 615–40.

work in the other article demonstrated some statistically significant relationships (both positive and negative) between prior judicial experience and what he conceptually and operationally defined as "adherence to precedent."[45] He also found a significant relationship between a tendency to dissent and whether or not a judge came from a "humble background."

In the former article Schmidhauser stated that.

> The fact that the Supreme Court tended to respond in a manner different from the sectional emphasis which became paramount in Congress after 1850 *very probably* reflected two influences—the felt need to preserve the integrity of the Court as an institutional guarantee to the justices of life tenure on good behavior.[46]

It is this type of statement which unfortunately minimizes the real value of this type of study and clearly highlights its inadequacies. On the other hand, the systematic, objective, quantifiable nature of the study has accumulated some significant information for the political behavioralist. Yet Schmidhauser risks having this value totally ignored or discounted because of the reckless jump to causation. How, on the basis of his study, can he state that "very probably" there is any reason or reasons which he can discern? He cannot. This, one would hope, is not the reason behind his systematic accumulation of data—to jump into the historian's shoes and make great inferential leaps to causation, and this in the face of his own warnings.

On the other hand, in his interpretation, we find another difficulty. For how can we be convinced that the judicial institution's guarantee of life tenure has some effect on personal values stemming from sectional background but not on those stemming from political party orientation? If he is stating that there is some relationship between this institutional insulation and background factors, fine. But how can he account for, on the basis

---

[45] "*Stare Decisis,* Dissent, and the Background of the Justices of the Supreme Court of the United States," *University of Toronto Law Review,* 14 (1962), 194–212.

[46] Schmidhauser, "Sectional Crisis . . .," p. 637 (emphasis added).

of his own study, its impact on one background variable and not on another? Again, through this type of study, he cannot.

FORWARD MOVEMENT

The major value to the work of Professors Nagel and Schmidhauser is that it is information (factual propositions) which is capable of being accumulated and stored and which, sometime in the near future, may serve as the building blocks for a significant generalization about such a relationship or such relationships. Though yet in a formative stage, this type of work appears to be another first step in the direction of attempting to understand the nature of the causative, or influential, or associational factors in judicial motivational structure through a use of social scientific theory and methods.

The latter Schmidhauser article has another and extremely important contribution. In fact it is a major, though implicit, move toward something that the judicial behavioral movement has almost totally overlooked in its studies to date, namely, that the judicial process is *judicial*. They have not yet made significant allowance for the fact that it may be a distinctive process with distinctive factors which ought to be studied as such. But this article by Schmidhauser, plus the second aforementioned article by Danelski, and another discussed below by Joseph Tanenhaus are the only ones to date to touch directly and substantially upon these factors in their study.

Schmidhauser has noted that there are such studiable elements as judicial role constraints. From the many that are considered to be effective to some degree he has selected adherence to precedent and the right to dissent in detail and at length if the judge so desires. Thus we have the first quantitative study of the relationship of any such variable with another variable. It is not overly important that in this case the role variable is the dependent one rather than an independent one. Neither is it ultimately important that Schmidhauser has severely limited its scope by insisting on an unambiguous referent, i.e., *express overruling* being tantamount to not adhering to precedent, as the only observable he would subject to quantification. This is justified by the pioneer role of this work. The significance of the study is in its recognition of this variable as being systematically observable and as being quantifiable. Danelski's work is significant in that he has attempted to study another unique judicial role function, i.e., the perception of the Chief Justice role as an independent variable effecting some judicial behavior. He *has* placed a judicial role variable in the position of being intervening for a policy result (though only in quantity and not in content). This too is a pioneer effort pushing on toward previously unrecognized frontiers. Tanenhaus' article is particularly significant in his attempt to isolate the major variables that comprise the judicial process.[47] His division is a threefold one: "The behavior of the Court at any given time is a product of three factors—the external, the institutional, and the personal."[48] Unfortunately for us again, he decided to hold the institutional factor constant and thus we do not actually have a study which affords us any insight into any of the theoretically distinctive features in which we are interested.

SUMMARY

A few concluding remarks at this point are designed to work a tightening effect and to prepare for the review of the writings of several noted legal scholars and judges.

To date, the political science analyst has scarcely begun to alter any method utilized in the study of the appellate decision-making process from its form as it had been previously applied by researchers in their study of other aspects of political or social processes. In fact, well known and useful concepts frequently have been twisted into unworkability, and greatly unwarranted generalizations have been made from limited data. These undesirable practices are understandable if it is true, as the literature

[47] Joseph Tanenhaus," Supreme Court Attitudes Toward Federal Administrative Agencies, 1947–56—An Application of Social Science Methods to the Study of the Judicial Process," *Vanderbilt Law Review*, 14 (1961), 473–502.
[48] Ibid., pp. 482–83.

seems to indicate, that explanation and understanding have actually been subordinated, in the main, to a certain mathematical
precision in description and to achievement of a certain level of
assumed prediction potential. This latter objective has been accomplished by emphasizing the objective manifestations of decision-making process (the votes) and avoiding the more internal
judicial ingredients.

Although it is certainly agreed that judicial decision-making
is similar to and *is* influenced by many of the same factors that
influence other phases of the policy-making process, it is also
quite possible (and is in fact often hypothesized to be so by
political scientists and others), that there are significant differences between the judicial and other political processes. In
fact, even the general political science literature has contained
much support for such a position. *But this view still remains to
be subjected to rigorous, systematic study.* The assumption which
has grounded much of the work thus far done by the political
behavioralists does little more than insist that a judge's personal
viewpoints on a particular aspect of the world will affect his
legal decision. The political behavioralist, by and large, has
given only lip-service to the judicial factors. He has hardly em-
barked upon the difficult task of separating out those features
which may have a significant enough impact upon the decision
so as to necessitate its description and to demand an accurate
understanding of its determinative role and perhaps of its functions or dysfunctions to society. Though movement has begun in
that direction, it is as yet perceivable only as distant rumblings.

It appears that it is mainly the work in jurisprudence, particularly that written by diverse strains of legal realists, which
approaches the problem of what these factors are and what
their interaction might be. Thus far it is the juridical scholar
who has gone it almost alone into the study of the nature of the
appellate judicial decision-making process as a possibly unique
phenomenon.

Thus the jurisprudent is primarily responsible for what little
understanding we now have of the *judicial* decision-making
process, if one really exists. These then are the primary con-

tributors toward a potential theory of judicial decision-making. Their work must be the source from which we can draw the conceptual prerequisites for any model of the process which will guide us in our quest for knowledge in this area. It is to them we must now turn.

Chapter II

Review of the Literature:
The Jurisprudents

AFTER reading through a good deal of the work of several outstanding jurisprudents on the nature of the judicial process, one may conclude that this material can be divided into two distinct segments, one of which deals with the theoretically peculiar nature of appellate judicial thinking (legal reasoning), and the other which covers the motivational or institutional factors which may interact with this thinking process. There is obviously no such real division in the appellate decision-making process itself. Concomitantly, it is difficult and highly artificial to make such a separation in the work of these jurisprudents, particularly since they do not make any such division explicitly. The distinction that we have suggested, as is the case with many classifications, is simply one of convenience for presentation and ease of analysis. It is possible that one could make a reasonably cogent case by arguing that there may be a difference in emphasis in a writer's total work or in an individual book or article of his, i.e., either upon the theoretical mechanics of the thought process itself or the institutional and other factors which interrelate with this process. At any rate, that is the basis of my categorization.

I noted in the Introduction that the legal scholar tends toward a far more normative posture than the political scientist-behavioralist. This is most noticeable in the first section of this chapter. The basic theme of most of the authors discussed in this section is that the judge or the judicial process *should* work in one way or another, i.e., the way in which they prescribe or not in the way which they proscribe. Culling the literature in search of a concept which is in general usage and which broadly includes the subject matter of all of these legal scholars, the most embracing concept to be found is that of role or judicial role. Therefore this concept would appear to be a suitable rubric under which to group the following works. This section, then, groups those authors who deal with (emphasize) the judicial decision-making role, that is, the appropriate role constraints upon the thought process. The second section of this chapter identifies those authors who discuss (1) the strains upon these role boundaries from motivational and personality sources and (2) other institutional supports for the role.

JUDICIAL THOUGHT PROCESS; THE JUDICIAL ROLE

Justice Owen J. Roberts may not rank among the greatest of the Supreme Court justices, but he left a legacy from which many political scientists and legal scholars have already derived abundant reward. For had not Justice Roberts written the majority decision in *U.S.* v. *Butler*,[1] many scholars of the recent past, and even of contemporary times, might have been forced back to Coke and Blackstone for target practice. Roberts has allowed these scholars both currency and importance.

As late as 1935, six members of the Supreme Court of the United States palpably supported the most archaic notions of what has been derisively called "slot-machine jurisprudence" and "mechanical jurisprudence."[2] However, even before the *Butler*

---

[1] 297 U.S. 1 (1936).

[2] What this means is best illustrated by some of Justice Roberts' remarks in *Butler:*

> There should be no misunderstanding as to the function of this court in such a case. It is sometimes said that the court assumes a power to overrule or control the action of the people's representatives. This is a misconception. The constitution is the su-

decision blatantly displayed the fact that the Supreme Court of the United States was still a bastion protecting these hoary notions, it had already been under attack from exceedingly respectable quarters including the Supreme Court bench itself (though in dissent) and the most hallowed and ivied of law-school halls.

The notion which came under most serious and steady attack was that the law was a body of general rules (major premise) from which, by a process of deduction (after the introduction of a minor premise), any specific controversy could be correctly solved through arriving at a more specific rule which would determine the proper immediate solution. This process (so it was claimed) produced a *certainty, continuity, and impartiality in the law*.[3] It was a view substantially based upon natural law beliefs. It was a view based upon the Cokean concept of the common law as "the perfection of reason" and as an established, accumu-

---

preme law of the land ordained and established by the people. All legislation must conform to the principles it lays down. When an act of Congress is appropriately challenged in the courts as not conforming to the constitutional mandate the judicial branch has only one duty,—to lay the article of the Constitution which is invoked beside the statute which is challenged and to decide whether the latter squares with the former. All the court does, or can do, is to announce its considered judgment upon the question. The only power it has, if such it may be called, is the power of judgment. 297 U.S. at 62.

[3] As late as 1959 we still find Judge Albert Tate of the First Circuit Court of Appeals (formerly of the Supreme Court of Louisiana) sadly recalling the erroneous concept of the judge's role that he entertained as a senior law student only a decade or so before:

If you had asked me . . . to describe the application of law through our judges—that is, to describe our machinery of justice —I think I would have imagined that a lawyer's function would be to feed the law he finds, through his brief and argument, into a sort of Univac, which after matching up the facts and legal principles against the law (comprised of statutes and the previously decided cases), would click out *the* correct answer. My concept of the judge was of the faceless intellect who simply matched up the opposing legal arguments and by a process of pure logic, with a few Latin maxims thrown in, enunciated the correct result. *Louisiana Law Review*, 19 (1959), 438, 439.

lated body of general rules which, through the passage of much time had gained a transcendental-like existence, apart from men, and which completely and wisely governed those men. The judge needed only to discover, through his legal skills, what the correct rule was in any given case. The judge needed only to follow the law. Thus, the decision was of law and not of man. It was truth through syllogism, not truth through the individual creative experience of the individual judge. This then, for the appellate judge, was the way he was supposed to make decisions in his official capacity. This was his decision-making role and underlies the Roberts view in *Butler*.

On the American front, Oliver Wendell Holmes[4] and John Chipman Gray[5] led the assault against this theory of what the thought-process of the judge should be, although Holmes and Gray were preceded by several renowned European jurisprudents. Widely quoted statements by Holmes such as, "The life of the law has not been logic; it has been experience" and "General propositions do not decide concrete cases" have almost become slogans. Yet they do underlie a theory of the law which has gained many adherents over the past several decades. This is that school of American jurisprudence known as legal realism. These Holmes aphorisms, along with his dissent in *Lochner* v. *New York*,[6] are the usual points of departure for most of the legal realist discourses against the Coke-Blackstone-Beale-Roberts fundamentalism.

Since the legal realists have helped to inject the concepts of society and personality into the study of the judicial decision-making process, they have also helped to project a clearer view of the actual contrast between other thought processes and the traditional theoretical formula for the legal thought process. This is so because the realists have managed to put the judicial decision-making process into the real world of men by showing its similarities with other mental processes. But they have thereby

---

[4] *The Common Law* (Boston: Little, Brown and Company, 1881).

[5] *The Nature and Sources of the Law* (New York: Columbia University Press, 1909).

[6] 198 U.S. 45 (1905).

highlighted the dissimilarities as well. Just what is the real nature of the difference as these men see it? And, more important, is there really a significant difference?

Just as the traditional economists of the 1930s found their most cherished concepts of rational man challenged by new schools of thought springing from the patent realities of the Depression, so did the traditional analytic jurisprudents find their mechanical model of the judge severely threatened. In fact, one would be hard pressed to find any strict adherents to the traditional theory today. But even the realists and neo-realists were at odds within their own groupings at the beginning—and remain so today. Their ideas as to the real or desired nature of the appellate decision-making process (and judicial process as a whole) are widely divergent. At one pole are those who would administer a mild injection of sociological and psychological ingredients into the system. They state that the judge must be made aware of the fact that he does and should take his own and the society's values and goals into account when making a decision. At the other pole we can find sweeping denunciations of all aspects of legal thinking coupled with exhortations to the judiciary to play honestly the role which they are said to play already, namely, that of the positive policy-maker. At this pole, the existence of precedent is seen as so much extra baggage. This section of the chapter is concerned with the work of the entire range of realists.

Divergence among the realists arises in the way in which each attempts to reconcile several factors: (1) the observable existence of the vast body of case-law, statutory law, and constitutional law; (2) that aspect of the judicial decision-making role which constrains the judge to apply the proper extant rule (or rules) to the specific case; (3) the fact that this cannot be done logically (by syllogism); and (4) the fact that the judge is a being with a human psyche who may have any number of varying opinions on the nature of the judicial role; the role of the judiciary in American society; and in fact, on all aspects of the social, political, and economic systems with which he has contact and which may be involved in any litigation before him. The many ways in which these factors are reconciled, however, can be collapsed into two main clusters. This is so because the realists are basically attempting to reconcile two poles of opinion.

The first pole is that of the traditionalists, whose normative position usually demands that the judge be strictly bound by precedent; the other pole is that of the positivists. Realists near or leaning towards the former pole see and recommend that the judge is and should be substantially bound by precedent, while those realists near or leaning towards the other pole see and recommend that the judge is hardly bound by precedent, but quite to the contrary, exercises and should exercise his own value preferences or those that he perceives to be in the best interests of the society. The former position can be labelled as the *precedent orientation* of the realists while the latter may be labelled as *situation orientation*. Since most realists are in the middle with simply a tendency toward one or the other orientation, it is usually very difficult to determine whether any particular legal scholar opts more for precedent or situation orientation. I shall not even try. The major reason for my reluctance is that I frequently find jurisprudents to be somewhat imprecise. Nonetheless, this somewhat stretched dichotomy does seem to help locate the problem with which these men are wrestling.

Pound

One of the outstanding legal minds of this century, Dean Roscoe Pound, lent his talents to an analysis of this problem. His view was that it was quite erroneous for the judiciary as well as the legal profession to entertain the belief that judges could

> Find the pre-appointed code pigeonhole for each concrete case, to put the case in hand into it by purely logical process and to formulate the result in a judgement . . . [and that] application is merely formulation in a judgement of the result obtained by analysis of the case and logical development of the premises contained in the reported decisions.[7]

---

[7] *An Introduction to the Philosophy of Law* (New Haven: Yale University Press, 1922), pp. 124–25.

Such a mechanistic view, in Pound's eye, was unrealistic and tended to perpetrate injustice. There was need, in law, for the court to keep in mind the necessity of "individualizing" the application of the law. And, according to Pound, to believe completely in the traditional view or in a totally individualistic approach was a great error since by its very nature the law demanded both orientations from the judge. To Pound, the world was divided into two areas: the world of conduct of human relations, and the world of things. The former included personal interaction, the latter included realty, fee simple, intestate succession and chattel mortgage. Pound believed that a mechanical, strict application in the latter and a loose, more individualistic application in the former would bring about the most just results.

> Philosophically, the apportionment of the field between rule and discretion which is suggested by the use of rules and of standards respectively in modern law has its basis in the respective fields of intelligence and intuition. Bergson tells us that the former is more adapted to the inorganic, the latter more to life. Likewise rules, where we proceed mechanically, are more adapted to property and to business transactions, and standards; where we proceed upon intuitions, are more adapted to human conduct and to the conduct of enterprises . . . Every promissory note is like every other. Every fee simple is like every other. Every distribution of assets repeats the conditions that have recurred since the Statute of Distributions. But no two cases of negligence have been alike or ever will be alike . . . For the certainty attained by mechanical application of fixed rules to human conduct has always been illusory.[8]

We could say, then, that Pound established a very neat dichotomy between precedent orientation and situation orientation for the judge. The former should be used in nonhuman relationships and the latter in human relationships. This is probably the clearest exhortation of when to use each orientation to be found in the jurisprudence literature.

---

[8] *Ibid.*, pp. 141–43.

Cardozo

Another leading American jurisprudent, Benjamin Cardozo, attacked this same problem about the same time as Pound. Although he was a prolific writer who covered many aspects of the nature of society, history, and philosophy, his basic theme was the judicial process, its nature, and its role in society. Again, it seems that much of his writing on this subject is reducible into our simplified category system.

Granting the existence of precedent and the changing nature of the world and society, what is the judicial role? To what extent should the judge be precedent-bound; to what extent should he be allowed to roam discretion-free? Our dichotomy fits quite well into the Cardozan way of thinking, for his view of the law and of life was that of conflicting tendencies. It was that of paradox.[9] And, in fact, according to him, "antithesis permeates the structure."[10] And so it is throughout his works in his overviews of the law, the legal system, and the nature of legal reasoning. For, as did Pound, so did Cardozo see different modes of thought which ought to and did characterize the legal thought process. To Cardozo the idea of a simplistic, deductive thought process was a poor joke and a dangerous illusion.[11] Rather, he saw desirable, constructive conflict in that which is and should be the real, creative thought process of the judge:

> Analysis alternates with synthesis; deduction with induction; reason with intuition. The whole in Geny's words is "a procedure extremely complex, and full of delicate nuances, all penetrated with casuistry and dialectics. . . ."[12]

---

[9] *Paradoxes of Legal Science* (New York: Columbia University Press, 1928).
> Deep beneath the surface of the legal system, hidden in the structure of the constituent atoms, are these attractions and repulsions, uniting and dissevering as in one unending paradox. "Fundamental opposites clash and are reconciled." (p. 7).

[10] *Ibid.*, p. 134.

[11] But, in Cardozo's mind, it was not the hoax and racket that Fred Rodell would have us believe. See, *Woe Unto You Lawyers!* (New York: Reynal and Hitchcock, 1939).

[12] Cardozo, *Growth of the Law* (New Haven: Yale University Press, 1924), p. 91. He is quoting from *Science et Technique en droit prive positif*, V. 1, p. 211, sec. 67.

The work in which Cardozo expounded at greatest length upon the judicial process, appropriately entitled *The Nature of the Judicial Process,* was a collection of lectures given at Yale in 1921.[13] Again we see the Cardozan concept of the judicial method as a potpourri of methods:

> Nothing is stable. Nothing absolute. All is fluid and changeable. There is an endless becoming. . . .
>
> In this perpetual flux, the problem which confronts the judge is in reality a twofold one; he must first extract from the precedents the underlying principle, the *ratio decidendi;* he must then determine the path or direction along which the principle is to move and develop, if it is not to wither and die. . . .
>
> The directive force of a principle may be exerted along the line of logical progression; this I will call the rule of analogy, or the method of philosophy; along the line of historical development; this I will call the method of evolution; along the line of the customs of the community; this I will call the method of tradition; along the line of justice, morals and social welfare, the *mores* of the day; and this I will call the method of sociology. . . .[14]

So it is with Cardozo, his fine mind attempting to isolate and describe the various factors involved in the very complex judicial method. But when we refine all this down to basic analytic components of strict adherence to precedent, rather than the desire to do justice in the immediate case, we are left uncertain. Should the judge be precedent-oriented or lean towards precedent orientation? Cardozo's answer is more yes than no; but that depends upon the case and its manifold situational conditions. This is the best we can do with Cardozo:

> . . . there is a good deal of discussion whether the rule of adherence to precedent ought to be abandoned altogether. I would not go so far myself. I think adherence to precedent should be the rule and not the exception. . . . I think that

---

[13] (New Haven: Yale University Press, 1921).
[14] *Ibid.,* pp. 28–31.

when a rule, after it has been duly tested by experience, has been found to be inconsistent with the sense of justice or with the social welfare, there should be less hesitation in frank avowal and full abandonment.[15]

This mixture of using precedent while being willing to do away with it when justice or growth so demand characterizes Cardozo and clearly distinguishes him from Pound. Cardozo's attempt at reconciliation of the two polar views is much more within the mainstream of thought in describing the process and, like the others, is also quite unclear as to when and to what extent precedent should direct the judge's decision.

Llewellyn and Cook

Karl Llewellyn, whom Jerome Frank once heralded as the "most brilliant of the rule skeptics," also saw the need for reconciling precedent, whether case, statutory, or constitutional, with the dictates of "justice," "right reason," "horse sense" and "wisdom" in arriving at the correct decision in a given case.[16] His statements on this topic seem much like Cardozo's. Thus we simply mention him as very close support for Cardozo; we need not lay down a barrage of specifics. The second section of this chapter contains detailed comment on Llewellyn.

Another well-known legal scholar who dichotomized all cases coming before a court in a way that manifests his desire for a similar reconciliation was Walter Wheeler Cook. He saw all cases as either "routine" or "new and unusual situations"[17] in relationship to extant precedent. In something akin to Pound's feelings on the matter, Cook believed that there were many cases of a routine nature, that is, where general legal principles quite clearly covered the immediate factual situation *sub judice* and where the judge could dispose of the case "without much

---

[15] *Ibid.*, pp. 149–50.

[16] *The Common Law Tradition* (Boston: Little, Brown and Company, 1960).

[17] See "The Logical and Legal Bases of the Conflicts of Law," *Yale Law Journal*, 33 (1929), 467–87; and " 'Substance' and 'Procedure' in the Conflicts of Law," *Yale Law Journal*, 42 (1933), 333.

thought." Other factual situations, being well beyond any clear control of any precedent, demanded an ability of the judge to employ the general outlines and wisdom of the precedent as a tool or instrument in arriving at the best possible result. It was, indeed, the judge's duty to create justice from his own skills and value perceptions.

Max Radin's distinction between logic and experience is similar and also fits within our scheme.[18] In some cases the former should be the judge's guide, and in other cases the latter ought to be used. In studying this area of jurisprudence, one soon begins to note the striking similarity of thought among the theorists.

Levi

However, coming further up to date, two major works on the nature of the judicial decision-making process stand out. The first of these is by Dean Edward Levi of the University of Chicago School of Law.[19] Levi's main point of dispute with the traditionalists—as well as with the extreme realists—is also on the way in which they treat logic in the judicial process. To Dean Levi, the former are too reverent and misguided while the latter are far too harsh and misguided. That logic in interaction with precedent has an important function in the process is obvious to Levi, but it is the *type* of logic in relation to existent precedent which he believes needs explication.

"Legal reasoning has a logic of its own,"[20] and Dean Levi, in

---

[18] *Law as Logic and Experience* (New Haven: Yale University Press, 1940).

[19] *Introduction to Legal Reasoning* (Chicago: University of Chicago Press, 1948).

[20] *Ibid.*, p. 4. Jerome Hall provides us with another excellent discussion of legal reasoning by analogy or analogical reasoning. This further illustrates the concept of legal reason as being an inductive rather than deductive type of thought process and the body of the law being a body of induced, growing, empirically based generalizations rather than of static, analytic, deduced generalizations. As Hall states:

> [reasoning by analogy] involves the search for similarities in fact-situations of known legal significance and fact situations whose legal significance is to be determined. When a lawyer

denoting it as "reasoning by example," demonstrates its mechanics by taking the reader through developmental lines of cases in the common law, statutory interpretation, and constitutional construction. Basically (and symbolically) it works as follows:

> A falls more appropriately in B than in C. It does so because A is more like D which is of B than it is like E which is of C. Since A is in B and B is in G (legal concept), then A is in G. But perhaps C is in G also. If so, then B is in a decisively different segment of G, because B is like H which is in G and has a different result than C.[21]

Levi's book is designed to show the importance of resorting to the existent case law as a method of resolving immediate disputes. His book *is* a monument to the proposition that courts make preposterous distinctions in deciding particular cases. But, it is *also* a master work that supports the notion that the law, as a set of concepts woven into principles of behavior, must and does gradually change as the empirical referents for the relevant legal concepts gradually change.

Substantially unlike much of the work already reviewed,

---

comes to court with an armful of law books, his purpose is to persuade the judge that the instant case must be decided in a certain way because very similar cases were decided that way in the past; and the principle of *stare decisis* enjoins continuity. The argument is similar to that employed in scientific method. If the inquiry concerns the existence of life on Mars, the scientist discovers and accumulates what he regards as similarities between Mars and Earth—the presence of oxygen, a certain range in temperature, and the like. He knows that life exists on Earth and, as the conditions of life increase on Mars, the probability rises that life exists there too. *So, also, as the similarity between the facts in the instant case and those in cases decided in the past increases, the duty to apply the same rules tends to become established.* On the other hand, important differences in the data compared diminish the analogy. The crucial question is whether the compared sets of facts are 'sufficiently alike.' *Living Law of Democratic Society* (Indianapolis: Bobbs-Merrill Company, 1949), pp. 47–48. (emphasis added)

[21] Levi, *op. cit.*, p. 4.

Levi's must is not explicitly a normative must at all, but rather, is empirically descriptive and seemingly based upon some type of implicit theory of society. Levi appears to see law as a support upon which it confidently moves forward. Even a lag is implied, but this is viewed as healthy instead of pernicious.

> Reasoning by example shows the decisive role which the common ideas of the society and the distinctions made by experts can have in shaping the law. The movement of common or expert concepts into the law may be followed. The concept is suggested in arguing difference or similarity in a brief, but it wins no approval from the court. The idea achieves standing in the society. It is suggested again to a court. The court this time reinterprets the prior case and in so doing adopts the rejected idea. In subsequent cases, the idea is given further definition and is tied to other ideas which have been accepted by the courts. It is now no longer the idea which was commonly held in the society. It becomes modified in subsequent cases. Ideas first rejected but which gradually have won acceptance now push what has become a legal category out of the system or convert it into something which may be its opposite. The process is one in which the ideas of the community win acceptance in the community, control legal decisions.[22]

So Levi presents the judge and the judicial process as a type of middleman, an arbiter in a forum, wielding established concepts against new concepts and yielding only to the latter upon their acceptance by the community. In our terms as set forth above (though unfortunately Levi does not fit in comfortably because of his relatively nonnormative approach), we might say that there is an emphasis upon precedent orientation, but that great care ought to be taken by the judge not to treat the precedent as immutable. It should simply be used, and is so used, as a guide and support. But again we cannot learn *when* the precedent ought to yield—we only learn of Levi's faith that it always has yielded and will probably continue to do so. The judge who would read Levi could not feel that he would have any basis for deciding that either the precedent or the immediate evidence and

---

[22] *Ibid.*

state of the societal view should be stressed in any specific case *sub judice.*

Hall

This same feeling that one gets in reading Pound, Cook, Cardozo, Llewellyn, and Levi will also grow out of a reading of Jerome Hall, another noted jurisprudent. Hall states that it is important to realize that the existence of an immense body of legal norms will unquestionably guide the decision-making behavior of the judge in many situations. As the clarity of a relevant rule or most directly relevant case becomes more obvious, it becomes increasingly incumbent upon the judge to apply such rule or case. Conversely, as the rule or case becomes less and less obviously related to the fact situation (to the extent of appearing to lack any guiding precedent), then it becomes increasingly more important for the judge to utilize his own discretion to decide the particular situation as best he can "in the most just way." It would seem that Hall believes that precedent may be clear enough to control the decision of the judge, and in such cases the judge should and does follow the line dictated by the rule. This is reminiscent of what we saw in Cook's work, e.g., routine equaling a clear precedential guide.

Hall clarifies this dimension in his description of precedent orientation. He also assails those legal scholars who, having seen the problems in blind allegiance to Cokean ideas on the nature of the Common Law and the judicial role, cannot see anything now but an unbridled use of judicial discretion:

> But the presence of many gaps in the legal system, the vagueness and ambiguity in the meaning of the rules, and the discretionary power to modify them, though they seriously undermine the traditional theory, do not support the extreme skepticism that law is subjective, uncontrolled caprice and that it is impossible to generalize legal meaning beyond the confines of each particular decision. For we must take account not only of the vagueness of the rules but also of their core of certainty; not only of the ambiguity of words but also of their relative univocality when defined in many decisions.[23]

---

[23] Hall, *op. cit.,* p. 45.

Wasserstrom

A recent book that is highly normative and that does present relatively explicit criteria on precedent versus situation orientation is *The Judicial Decision* by Richard Wasserstrom, Professor of Law and Philosophy at the Stanford Law School.[24] In fact Wasserstrom's effort is bent entirely towards the study of the various judicial decisional procedures in the hope that he will be able to suggest that procedure which will afford "maximum effect to the needs, desires, interests, and aspirations of the members of the society of which it is a part."[25]

His two major categories of judicial procedure are precedent and equity. This should strike a most familiar chord by now. Wasserstrom sees the use of logic as a genuine restraint on the free vent of the personal values of the judge, although he believes that the latter does influence the decision. He expressly denies the old, deductive logic argument. But—and this is a key point in Wasserstrom's work—no matter what the actual reason behind the choice of decision, the judge is compelled to *justify* his decision logically.

> . . . there do not seem to be any very persuasive reasons for believing that the adoption of some procedures of justification would not have an important effect upon the way in which courts decide particular cases.[26]

In essence, what he means by a logical justification is simply that there must be, even though *post hoc,* some deductive line of thought available in order for a judge to hold in a certain way. As long as he could deduce the decision from more general rules, then the particular decision is justifiable. This is, of course, quite distinguishable from the traditionalist view that the decision was actually reached through the deduction and is "correct" or "just" thereby. Equity is seen as the appeal, by the judge, to something other than reason in the hope that justice will be served. The

---

[24] (Stanford: Stanford University Press, 1961).
[25] *Ibid.,* p. 10.
[26] *Ibid.,* p. 31.

usual source of the just decision, in the equitable procedure, is "intuition." Shades of Bergson and Pound!

Wasserstrom's final suggestion to us should not be surprising. He holds that the best procedure is a "two-level procedure of legal justification,"

> . . . an attempt to bring into some kind of systematic program the more desirable features of alternative modes of decision. The two-level procedure is like the precedential decision procedure in its insistence that individual decisions be justifiable by appeal to relevant legal rules. It is unlike the precedential procedure in its insistence that the presence of an existing rule is not the sufficient justification for a decision. The two-level procedure is like the equitable decision procedure in its requirement that considerations of justice or utility be relevant to the justification of decisions. It is unlike the equitable decision procedure in its requirement that considerations of justice or utility be relevant to the justification of rules rather than particular decisions.[27]

Wechsler-Pollok-Hart versus Miller-Howell

This part of our survey is best brought up to date by reviewing the essentials of a recent law review debate carried on by several prominent members of the law-teaching profession. It is one of the little ironies of academia, as of politics and war, that strange and somewhat hostile bedfellows are sometimes made. Oddly enough, three men whom we now classify together as representing one position were previously the participants in a debate among themselves. But the two authors of another article noted a vital rapport among the three that fits well into the development of what we have heretofore observed.

Herbert Wechsler, Louis H. Pollok and Henry Hart engaged in a widely read law review feud in 1959.[28] The issue at hand

---

[27] *Ibid.*, p. 171.

[28] Herbert Wechsler, "Toward Neutral Principles of Constitutional Law," *Harvard Law Review*, 73 (1959) 1; Louis H. Pollok, "Racial Discrimination and Judicial Integrity: A Reply to Professor Wechsler," *University of Pennsylvania Law Review*, 108 (1959) 108; Henry M. Hart, "Forward: The Time Chart of the Justices," *Harvard Law Review*, 73 (1959) 84.

seemed to boil down to a questioning of the extent to which the Supreme Court, in the segregation cases, abandoned the traditional (or traditionalistic) role requirement and relied instead upon the "neutral principles" of constitutional law. It would seem that all three can be comfortably placed in the realist camp since they accept the necessity of tempering the amorphous, highly abstract principles of the law as the times demand. Wechsler's "neutral principles" are probably best described as the general trends of the past. Yet, he does not want to see the law *develop* in a *trend sequence*, but only, as Wasserstrom might say, with reasoned justification. This appears to be what Wechsler means by a "principled decision":

> The courts have both the title and the duty when a case is properly before them to review the actions in the light of constitutional provisions, even though the action involves value choices, as invariably action does. In doing so, however, they are bound to function otherwise than as a naked power organ; they participate as courts of law. This calls for facing how determinations of this kind can be asserted to have any legal quality. The answer, I suggest, inheres primarily in that they are—or are obliged to be—entirely principled. A principled decision, in the sense I have in mind, is one that rests on reasons with respect to all the issues in the case, reasons that in their generality and their neutrality transcend any immediate result that is involved. . . .[29]

The fact that Professor Wechsler does indeed envisage and does in fact desire alterations in his neutral principles is more explicitly stated in another part of his article:

> It is difficult for me to think the Fourth Amendment freezes for all time the common law of search and of arrest as it prevailed when the amendment was adopted, whatever the exigencies of police problems may now be or may become.[30]

---

[29] The Wechsler article is also contained as one of a series of articles that comprises his recent book, *Principles, Politics, and Fundamental Law* (Cambridge: Harvard University Press, 1961). This quotation can be found therein at p. 27.

[30] *Ibid.*

Although Professors Pollok and Hart manage to join issue upon other aspects of the Wechsler piece, it does seem as though they all do believe that there may exist a body of neutral principles or impersonal rules against which a judge must refer in making his decision in a particular case.

It is at this point that Professors Arthur S. Miller and Ronald Howell voice deep disagreement (although at times the exact nature of this disagreement is confused).[31] By the time one finishes reading the Miller-Howell argument, it is reasonably clear that their essay presents one of the most vehemently positivistic, anti-precedent orientation and pro-situation orientation positions to be found anywhere in the jurisprudential literature.[32] They begin by discussing the impossibility of any legal objectivity due to precedent. In their words:

> The first point we want to make is this: Adherence to neutral principles, in the sense of principles which do not refer to value choices, is impossible in the constitutional adjudicative process (we limit ourselves to constitutional adjudication at this time, although much of what is said here is applicable to litigation generally). Strive as he might, no participant in that process can be neutral. . . . Principles, whatever they might be, are abstractions, and it is the worst sort of anthropomorphism to attribute human characteristics to them. Neutrality, if it means anything, can only refer to the thought processes of identifiable human beings. Principles cannot be neutral or biased or prejudiced or impersonal—obviously. The choices that are made by judges in constitutional cases always involve consequences, thus making value choice unavoidable.[33]

They then launch into a lengthy exploration of the concept of neutrality or objectivity as it is used in many other disciplines.

---

[31] Arthur S. Miller and Ronald F. Howell, "The Myth of Neutrality in Constitutional Adjudication," *University of Chicago Law Review,* 27 (1960) 661.

[32] These two authors, though, do bow in approval of and in appreciation to Alexander M. Pekelis's *Law and Social Action* (Ithaca: Cornell University Press, 1950).

[33] Miller and Howell, *op. cit.,* p. 664.

They attempt to demonstrate to us that biologists, physicists, and various social scientists all agree that value preferences influence their own studies and decisions. From this proposition the coauthors then present a corollary which states that when a choice among competing values is made in a courtroom situation, the decision is the outcome of the entire biography and heredity of the individual judge and not of objective criteria. Whatever objectivity they may ascribe to the outcome of the judicial process is not to be attributed to the existence of any abstract principles of law. To claim such is simply, in their eyes, naive and only leads to an obfuscation of the real factors that may bring about objectivity.

> What we suggest is that [Wechsler's] quest for neutrality is fruitless. In the interest-balancing procedure of constitutional adjudication, neutrality has no place, objectivity is achievable only in part, and impartiality is more of an aspiration than a fact—although certainly possible in some degree. In making choices among competing values, the Justices of the Supreme Court are themselves guided by value preferences. Any reference to neutral or impersonal principles is, accordingly, little more than a call for a return to a mechanistic jurisprudence and for a jurisprudence of non-disclosure as well as an attempted denial of the teleological aspects of decision, wherever made. . . . [34]

Those factors that Miller and Howell indicate as being related to some degree of objectivity in the judicial decision-making process are inherent only in the institution's trappings and status. They speak of the effects of the use of the black robe and the general esteem in which the judge is held. Studies supporting the occupational prestige level of the judges could have been cited but were not. We are left to accept on faith that the traditional view of the effectiveness of the judicial garb does indeed hold a magical quality for the judge himself.

The two professors do appear to run into a serious inconsistency later in their paper. They state that there is much greater

---

[34] *Ibid.*, p. 671.

stability in other sectors of American law than in constitutional law, and that this is because of the existence of more "fairly clear precedents."[35] Once again, the spectors of Cook and Hall loom large. Does this not seem to admit that, along with the Hall view discussed above, the greater the clarity of precedent, the greater the effect of it upon the judge in his selection of alternatives? And is not the next step then to claim that if the judge is led by the clear precedent to decide as it dictates, that this is basically tending toward an objectivity in the decision because of it? But nothing more is said along these lines.

The panaceae suggested by Miller and Howell are (1) for the judiciary to practice openness by declaring their values rather than deciding upon them covertly and disguising their decision with words like "objectivity"; and (2) for judges to make conscious choices among alternatives by using a scientific method to choose those means to achieve their own personal goal-preference. This they call "teleological jurisprudence." This is, by their own statements, the Lasswell-MacDougal policy-making orientation for the judge.[36] It is quite clearly a call to the judiciary to make policy in much the same manner as any other policy-making branch in the governmental system in order to meet the new needs of the society. Their final stand, then, is a blatant, total, situation orientation.

> Reason, Hart to the contrary, in these instances, if not in others, is emphatically not "the life of the law"; rather it is the language of political battle. And the Court is a power organ, which aids in the shaping of community values whether avowedly so as in the hands of a Douglas or whether abashedly so when Frankfurter seeks to convince us that he is an apostle of "self-restraint." Whatever its decision—even a denial of certiorari or taking refuge within the doughy contours of "political questions"—the Court is institutionally a part of a government with affirmative orientation: In a welfare state, it is also concerned with welfare. The only question is whether is should be *out-*

---

[35] *Ibid.*, p. 677.

[36] Myres D. MacDougal and associates, *Studies in the World Public Order* (New Haven: Yale University Press, 1960).

wardly so, and whether it should try to be so systematically, rather than in a helter-skelter manner.[37]

Not only is their description of and exhortation to a complete situation orientation, but it is a loud, brazen proclamation of such. Miller and Howell have cast Wechsler into a traditionalist form, where he does not belong. Wechsler is admittedly quite within the realist fold—it is Miller and Howell who do not see their delinquency. Their argument is most interestingly and logically developed, but one does feel compelled to ask these two men (although it is by and large irrelevant to this paper) what reasons they would advance for allowing the Court to continue to exist in its present form and institutional position. Also, one would be curious to know why they believe that the public would support or even tolerate such a modern version of the Nocturnal Council.

Be this as it may, the Miller-Howell position does bring us full cycle to an extreme positivistic view. And since they do discuss sartorial jurisprudence and judicial prestige, we are led directly into the next section of this chapter, namely, that in which we shall take a somewhat briefer look at some of the work done on the actual interrelationships between the judge's personality (and perhaps other motivational factors), the institutional characteristics of the judiciary, and the judicial role. For it is in this latter type of study, in relation to the work of the legal scholars just discussed, that we begin to recognize the important steps already taken towards isolating the key elements which we need to understand separately and in interaction if we are ever to understand the nature of what is considered to be the judicial process.

MOTIVATIONAL AND INSTITUTIONAL FACTORS

Many of the legal commentators who recognize the importance of understanding the motivational-institutional factors that affect the judge have themselves been judges. We have already

---

[37] Miller and Howell, *op. cit.*, p. 689.

discussed some of their works in detail. Of course, we do not mean to imply that all or even most legal scholars conceive of the study of the psychological processes of a judge as being worthy of more than footnote reference.[38] But almost all those who would be considered legal realists do.

Bernard Schientag, as a justice of the Supreme Court of the State of New York, exhorted fellow lawyers to comprehend the importance of realizing that the judge is not manufactured by the legal engineers of IBM, and that comprehensive and intensive study of the judge's psychological process would bear important fruit.

> The personality of the judge, likewise, must be studied in light of psychological principles which, in large measure, apply to him as they do to all human beings. We must recognize the importance of the judicial personality with its strength and its weaknesses and endeavor to utilize the strength and minimize the weaknesses.[39]

Justice Schientag then set forth what he considered to be eight cardinal judicial virtues: independence, courtesy and patience, dignity: the judge's sense of humor, openmindedness, impartiality, thoroughness and decisiveness, an understanding heart, and social consciousness. In discussing each "virtue" he attempted to establish relationships between it and the judge's

---

[38] A most prominent advocate of this position is Professor Bernard Schwartz of New York University Law School and the Committee on Legislative Oversight fame. (See, *The Professor and the Committee* (New York: Alfred A. Knopf, 1959)). Schwartz states in his book *The Supreme Court: Constitutional Revolution in Retrospect* (New York: The Ronald Press, 1957) that:

> The present book has been based upon the view that, even in a splintered Supreme Court there are certain broad principles that have dominated the Court's work. It is this which makes possible an analysis of the high tribunal's jurisprudence from an institutional point of view without more than a passing reference to the individual personalities of the justices. (p. 344)

[39] Bernard Schientag, *The Personality of the Judge* (New York: The Association of the Bar of the City of New York, Committee on Post-Admission Legal Education, 1944), pp. 96–97.

personality. Although this study tends toward an oversimplification of psychological concepts and theories, the general idea involved becomes particularly interesting if one discards the concept of virtue and reworks the various components in terms of role theory. But more on this point subsequently.

Cardozo has also expressed his cognizance of the importance of subconscious factors on the judicial decision:

> Deep below consciousness are other forces, the likes and dislikes, the predilections and the prejudices, the complex of instincts and emotions and habits and convictions, which make the man, whether litigant or judge.[40]

Unfortunately though, Cardozo stated that he had not the opportunity to penetrate any deeper but wanted to note the existence of the problem. One legal analyst has even gone as far as to state that "the judge is exposed more than any other thinker to emotional influences" and that misconceptions "produced by emotion are felt most often and easiest in the field of legal thinking."[41] This, clearly, is the extreme position, but it lends support to the aforementioned hypothesis on the possible differences between the appellate decision-making process and the policy processes of the other areas of the political system.

Jerome Frank is probably the outstanding illustration of a legal scholar who was intensely aware of the wide range of problems rooted in a psychologically based theory of judicial decision-making, who engaged in analysis of those problems, and who even managed to suggest pertinent remedies.[42] It must also

---

[40] *The Nature of the Judicial Process*, p. 167.

[41] Wurzel, "Methods of Juridical Thinking," *Science of Legal Method*.

[42] Judge Frank makes a definite distinction between the decision-making process at the trial and appellate levels. To Frank, the trial judge has the more difficult chore as well as the fundamental one. Despite the distinction, the writer believes that a fair brief can be made arguing that particularly in the similarity of much of the legal reasoning process, the judging function is essentially the same. See Frank's article "Judicial Fact-Finding and Psychology," *Ohio State Law Journal*, 14 (1953) 183; and his two classics: *Law and the Modern Mind* (New York: Coward-McCann, 1930) and *Courts on Trial* (Princeton: Princeton University Press, 1950).

be emphasized that he contributed much directly to the study of the judicial decision-making process as discussed in the earlier portions of this chapter. But he was most deeply concerned over the fact that judges, because of their biases and prejudices, must have a distorted perception of fact, as well as of the law directly relevant or desirable for application. He was the first major fact-skeptic (to use his own phrase) of the realist movement. Frank went so far as to suggest that judges and justice may be best served by the attachment of a psychiatrist to each court who would be available for consultation by any judge who believed he was experiencing too high a level of anxiety. This consultation, Frank believed, might allow for relatively objective perception of the facts and law that day. But all of this, again, is simply the recognition of the reality that judges have psychic-emotional processes which need to be studied and understood in order to comprehend why any decision is made.

Karl Llewellyn's last major work, *The Common Law Tradition,* is a notable contribution to the literature dealing with the institutional context of the judicial process.[43] Briefly, Professor Llewellyn's theory involves two main elements which when combined are deemed to result in a certainty of outcome of the process: a "reckonability" of the content of the decision. The elements are (1) fourteen "stabilizing factors" and (2) the use of horse sense and right reason to manipulate precedent justly so as to reach the correct or best decision. Several of the stabilizing factors mentioned are: the judge's legal training and use of established precedent; the belief in the existence of one single, "right" answer; group decision; and the judicial office.[44] Many of the fourteen elements can be reduced to subclasses of the two major judicially distinguishing thought factors discussed above in the first section.

Unfortunately, however, Professor Llewellyn jumps off in midstream and neglects to extrapolate upon the nature of the inter-

---

[43] Note 16, *supra.*

[44] See the section entitled' "Major Steadying Factors in Our Appellate Courts," pp. 19–61.

relationship between these factors, the extent and nature of overlap, the probable varying degrees of importance between the elements, as well as many other problems raised by a mere listing. Bare mention and a brief description of each element is deemed to be sufficient by Llewellyn. Nevertheless, we do find what is probably the most elaborate analysis of the nature of those discrete elements that substantially contribute to a constraint upon a judge (as contrasted with all other types of policy-makers) in arriving at a choice between alternatives.

Some judges are willing to discuss such factors at length. For instance, Justice Tom Clark, in a personal interview, mentioned several other factors which lead to more objective thinking on the part of the judge. First, he is impressed by the personal isolation in which the judge finds himself. For instance he said, "My old friends hardly ever come by anymore or call me up when they are in Washington." This, he noted, was in sharp contrast to their behavior when he was Attorney General of the United States. Second, he observed that he took each case under much greater deliberation as a justice than he had as Attorney General. In the latter role "the courts could reverse any errors we made." This luxury for the conscience doesn't exist for a Supreme Court justice. Of course, we are assuming a relationship between greater deliberation and greater impartiality. But this seems to be what Justice Clark was getting at when he stated that decisions "weighed more heavily" as a justice than those as Attorney General. All of this is of obvious interest to us in our endeavor to isolate the variables that may distinguish the judicial process from any other.

In this portion of this book, we have seen that legal academicians and appellate judges-jurisprudents have produced some broad, theoretical material which could lay a basic framework for much intensive, behaviorally-based research. But they have not designed nor conducted any empirical research which could yield any quantifiable information about the possible peculiar nature of the appellate decision-making process. There has been no work accomplished that would avail us of empirically verified, motivationally-oriented propositions that are the *sine qua non* for constructing hard theory on the nature of that process. Yet the production of much material *leading towards* useful concepts, provocative propositions, and a general, though implicit, empirical theoretical scheme of the nature of the judicial decision-making process is not something to be ignored; it should be utilized by those who are interested in this area.

SUMMARY

Decisions of any policy-maker are the result of an interaction of many factors. Two of the most important are his own comprehensive value system and his view of the role of the policy-maker which he is playing. Obviously judges, as well as administrators, cabinet members, etc., have a deeply embedded, complex system of social, economic, and political values. However, the different institutional environments in which these men function may cause them to maintain different expectations as to their degree of freedom in exercising these values in regard to any decision they may be called upon to make. This statement is in accord with the leading works on the nature of policy decision-making processes.[45] Thus, if a man believes that his personal values are *not supposed to be relevant to decision in his role,* can we categorically state that his belief will *not* affect his behavior in relationship to the maximum attainment of any such values through his decision? Can we state that the values are the whole cause simply because we find a partial relationship? Of course he may rationalize in order to bring his values to a decisional fruition, etc., but this would remain to be seen.

[45] See Richard C. Snyder, "A Decision-Making Approach to the Study of Political Phenomena," in Roland Young (ed), *Approaches to the Study of Politics* (Evanston: Northwestern University Press, 1958). Snyder discusses three main determinants of decision-making behavior: (1) spheres of competence, (2) communication and information, and (3) motivation. Our concepts of role and values seem to fit within Snyder's categories (1) and (3) respectively. The variable of clear precedent, discussed in detail later in the text would probably fit well within Snyder's second category. See also, Snyder, H. W. Bruck, and Burton Sapin, *Foreign Policy Decision Making* (New York: The Free Press of Glencoe, 1962).

In this chapter we have surveyed the work of some of the leading American jurisprudents which presents their views on what they consider to be the desirable interrelationship between the judge's personal notions of what this society may need (as colored by his social, economic, and political values), the existence of the law (the precedent), judicial role (the judge's thought process), and the judicial institutional environment. We have seen that there is a great divergence in the content of their recommendations. Yet, it is apparent that they all do handle the same key elements in their treatment of the subject matter. Moreover, the whole process could be said to be seen by them to pivot on one major concept, judicial role. To comprehend the detailed, exact nature of that concept in its interaction with the other named major elements appears to be at least one key to understanding the judicial process. It is upon this task that we now embark.

Chapter III

Explication of Judicial Role
and a First Theoretical Step

EXPLICATION

The major proposition to be studied in this book involves a definition of the appellate judge's own view of the nature of his judicial or professional position. This particularly includes the belief that the dictates of relevant law, when brought to his attention, ought to be explicitly followed. It is proposed that this limits the effect of the judge's own substantive values as a determining factor in decision-making when the decision is made within a judicial institutional setting. Political scientists who study the American appellate judicial process generally agree that this consideration makes up at least a portion of their theory of the judicial process. *Even* the political science judicial behavioralists, through implication and attempt at refutation, *mention* this decision-making norm (in their desire to tell us what they choose to ignore). We have also noted that all common-law jurisprudents deal with this proposition in various ways and to varying degrees. Thus, it can be said that the *entire* body of outstanding relevant theory on various aspects of the American appellate judicial system treats this idea—either positively or negatively. Our desire is to learn whether, and if so just how much and in what ways, this proposition may actually be true and would thus distinguish such a decisional process from that where the role picture offers no such constraints on decision-making and, in fact, may even encourage personal value implementation, e.g., Burke's theory of legislative representation.

A first step in clearing up the reigning confusion on this topic is to attempt an explication of the pivotal concept of judicial role.[1] We will tackle that problem first. Then we will deal with the interrelationships of the several theoretical components and their explication.

Role and Judicial Role

The concept of role is one which has been a favorite of sociologists and social psychologists for studying everything from doctors and army officers to school superintendents. But despite its frequent utilization it cannot be borrowed for a study of the judicial process in an unchanged form. To do that would be to continue along the same path that most political behavioralists have already trod—and which has often led astray. Our problem is to try to arrive at a satisfactory conceptual and operational definition of judicial role in order to assist us in our search towards an understanding of the appellate judicial process. To do this systematically, we will first establish the broadest contours of the conceptual definition of role. Secondly, we will demonstrate the nature of the conceptual peculiarities of our type of role (judicial role). Lastly, we will deal with the problem of defining that concept more precisely.

One could go into a lengthy outpouring of the views of some of the more prominent scholars in the fields of anthropology, social psychology, and sociology who have formulated detailed and theoretically integrated definitions of role, e.g., Linton, G. H. Mead, Kluckhohn, Parsons, Davis, Newcomb, Cottrell, and Sar-

---

[1] For the purposes of this study, we are limiting the study of judicial role to that as it exists in the United States. It is believed that there may be many variations of the concept of judicial role to be found throughout the common-law world. Moreover, the differences in the perceived judicial role may well be even more dramatic when a comparison between the role of the common law judge and the civil law judge is eventually effectuated.

bin. But this would not advance our purposes directly.[2] Research results in the area of judicial decision-making would seem to be facilitated by a minimization of concern over the comprehensive, objective, prescriptive elements dwelt on by most people who use the concept of role. It is even questionable whether any effective ones exist which apply to the judicial process. Indeed, the concept of judicial role as delineated by the jurisprudent is quite different.

The most satisfactory way of explicating the key differences between related general concepts would be to examine work which has dealt with a more concrete set of elements of both concepts. If empirical work has only been done on one, then it would seem to be best to turn to that work. Yet a review of empirical level role studies discloses that they cannot assist us in understanding the role-to-decision relationship in the judiciary. Our review of this literature, then, must simply be an attempt to establish the relevant distinctions at this more specific level in order to clarify the pertinent differences between the more widely accepted definition of role and the jurisprudential notion of role.

Instead of accomplishing this through a grandiose survey of all of the social science empirical research utilizing the concept of role, we will, simply for the sake of expedience, limit our examination to two recent landmark studies. These two studies are proximate enough to the problem under scrutiny to lend further clarity to a definition of the relevant differences. In this way we will demarcate most sharply the divergence between our subsequently proposed approach and the nature of the utilization of the role concept by others. All of this provides the backdrop for the particular approaches suggested in the next section.

Explorations in Role Analysis

The first major work we will investigate is *Explorations in Role Analysis* by Neal Gross, Ward S. Mason, and Alexander

---

[2] For those who are interested in the differences among their highly conceptual definitions, see Lionel J. Neiman and James W. Hughes, "The Problems of the Concept of Role—A Re-survey of the Literature," *Social Forces*, 30 (1951), 141–49. Also, there is an excellent recapitulation of this work in Chapter 2 of the Gross, et al., work (see following footnote).

McEachern.[3] This book subtitled: *Studies of the School Superintendency Role,* is one of several publications which have reported or will report the findings of the School for Executive Studies, a research program initiated at Harvard University in 1952.

Unfortunately for our purposes, this book, despite its great scope and depth, does not touch upon the expectations which might relate to the particular professional decision-making process as a thought process, e.g., the legal mind, the scientific mind, etc. In other words, the principal focus in the superintendency study is not of the superintendent's professional thinking process. For example, there is no attention whatsoever given to describing and analyzing the criteria by which a superintendent is to judge the work of the teachers under his jurisdiction. Instead the study directs its scrutiny towards the *overt, physical-behavior* expectations of the school superintendent: How should a superintendent *act* toward others, e.g., mothers of students, principals, school board members, colleagues, teachers, etc.? The very concept of role is defined in terms of expected physical behavior of the incumbents of one position toward incumbents of other positions in given situational contexts. This is very much the way in which social scientists of all persuasions have employed the concept.

For us, however, it is not important in designing a study strategy which helps advance towards an understanding of the judicial process to determine what role definers (the judges themselves) say or believe a judge must *do* in various situational contexts. Perhaps this is important for those who would study many of the diverse policy-making roles—but it is not important for those interested in the judge, *qua* decision-maker. We need not be concerned with what a judge must do in relation to lawyers in court, lawyers at professional association meetings, other judges at a conference, or politicians at a political rally. Such data, though undoubtedly interesting and by and large unstudied, is not an aspect of the judicial role that would appear to bear significantly upon the appellate judicial decision, and that is what we are interested in understanding.

---

[3] (New York: John Wiley and Sons, 1958).

It does not seem to be an unwarranted stretching of the concept of role to consider the *thought process as a behavior* subject to role constraints. This would necessitate the spelling out of an expectation that the encumbent of the position would adhere to a certain carefully delineated mental process. But is there a consensus as to what the judicial mental process ought to be? Can we determine the nature of that consensus? Gross demonstrates•that the frequent assumption that there is a consensus among role definers on expectations for the behavior of a position holder will not always stand up to empirical investigation. His findings are convincing. However, knowledge of the degrees of role consensus on the judicial decision-making role and of the major variances or divergences from consensus on certain aspects of such role expectation could prove to be an important variable for some significant propositions. In light of the material reviewed earlier on the nature of the judicial process and legal reasoning, it would not be too surprising to find, upon an analysis of the data we might get from the whole range of role-definers, that two major clusters or variations would appear: to guide them in making their decisions, judges should be either precedent-oriented or situation-oriented.

The Legislative System

Explorations in Role Analysis provides us with an excellent example of the specific role elements which we do *not* need to describe or relate. As this is representative of the vast majority of work done in the social sciences with the concept of role, the uniqueness of the task which still confronts us should now be quite clear. However, another recent study which has developed extensive operations on the support of a policy-making role is *The Legislative System* by John C. Wahlke, Heinz Eulau, William Buchanan and LeRoy C. Ferguson.[4] As its title indicates, its *substance* is closer to our area of interest than that of the school superintendency study. But this merit is minimal when contrasted with that inherent in other differences between this study and that of Gross, *et al.* For, *The Legislative System* is a modern

---

[4] (New York: John Wiley and Sons, 1962).

classic of political science which contributes much to the use of this book's own suggested conceptual approach. It also provides us with another specific dissimilarity in type of role expectation which will further highlight and outline that which lies within the boundaries of what we believe is essential to study in order to understand the mechanics of the appellate judicial process.

One key contribution of this book is the reinforcement of the view, through concrete research, that the concept of role may have a unique quality for being a foundation for describing and analyzing human behavior in policy-making institutional contexts (processes). The findings presented are a testimonial to the concept's utility in organizing data on a governmental subsystem into meaningful categories. It is an attempt to make a sharp demarcation of the parameters of the legislative role. But, in very much the same fashion, the concept of legislative role has been the subject of much varied conceptualization, much impressionism, and little operationalization. Its second major contribution, then, comes in producing a hard policy-making role concept. The process gone through to achieve this (questionnaires, charts, etc.) has paved the way for much more research employing this concept.

To be sure, *much* of *The Legislative System* is devoted to describing the role expectations of *overt, physical behavior* of the state legislator, just as the Gross work does *exclusively* with the school superintendent. As an illustration, two conceptual elements of the legislative role, "performance of obligation" and "self restraint," are operationalized as questionnaire items (respectively) as follows: "Keep your word," and "Don't talk too much." Other aspects of legislative role behavior which are treated by Wahlke *et al.* are what is expected of legislators as being subject matter experts.[5] But perhaps the greatest forward step taken in their book, from our point of view, is that this study has begun to develop the notion of role and role expectation in relationship to a decision-making process *qua* the thought process of the policy-maker. *And it does this operationally.*

---

[5] *Ibid.*, Ch. 9.

In Chapter 12 we find the fruits of an attempt to describe as accurately as possible the various factors which a legislator keeps in mind in making policy decisions. Many questions are posed and answered on the thought process of the legislator. What does a legislator consider himself to be as a policy-maker? Should he just meet each issue as an individual human being and decide in his own discretion, what is good, right, correct, or valuable? Or, on the other hand, should he be a barometer in the legislature of what the climate of his constituency might be on any given issue?

The authors have divided the thought process (decision-making) role orientations into three categories: trustee, delegate and politico.[6]

The trustee is the Burkean ideal:

[He] sees himself as a free agent in that, as a premise of his decision-making behavior, he claims to follow what he considers right or just, his convictions and principles, the dictates of his conscience.[7]

The delegate is the constituency's conduit, particularly one type of delegate:

Finally, there is the representative in the delegate role who not only feels he should follow instructions, *but who also believes that he should do so even if these instructions are explicitly counter to his own judgement or principles.*[8]

The politico is a hybrid between the trustee and the delegate. As one politico was quoted as saying:

There is an age-old question—should I vote according to my convictions, or according to the people back home? I think I should follow my convictions but consider the people back home.[9]

---

[6] *Ibid.*, p. 272.
[7] *Ibid.*
[8] *Ibid.*, p. 276 (emphasis added).
[9] *Ibid.*, p. 279.

By now, the definition of the delegate ought to tweak a responsive chord in the reader. After all, doesn't it seem to be very much akin to the notion of personal value impartiality or objectivity which we have earmarked as the chief theoretically distinguishing characteristic between the judicial process and all other policy-making processes? Is it not so that if the authors of *The Legislative System* are correct, we would have no *distinctive* process to study? In fact, the authors of that book have indicated this apparent similarity of process quite explicitly:

> It may well be that, as in the judicial process, legislators are guided by precedents, and in the formal sense of legislative process, they certainly are.[10]

Placing this notion into the frame of reference developed earlier poses two key questions: (1) Is the legislator's adherence to the public interest, the general welfare, and the commonweal in making his decision similar to the value-constraint nature of the theoretical judicial role? (2) Is the legislator who determines through elaborate research that his constituents desire a policy other than that which he would personally choose and who then votes as his constituency would have it because he believes he is their delegate, essentially going through the same process that the theoretical judge goes through? The answer to the first question is No. The answer to the second question is Yes.

The first situation (answered in the negative), where the legislator binds his values by making them conform to the general welfare etc., is an illusory constraint. This is due to its fundamentally *subjective* quality. No extant *objective* constraint really exists to bind his decision. It is common knowledge that one's own general value posture is closely related to one's view of the common good. This is no more of a constraint upon the legislator than the constraint which all judges impose upon themselves to be just. But this notion of being just is neither the essence nor the most important part of the judicial role constraint in which we are interested.

---

[10] *Ibid.*, p. 237.

The second question (answered affirmatively) does involve an external value system which the judge's concept of role plus the theoretical concept of role may compel him to heed. Though it is true that the discovery of the objective and real nature of the constituency's wishes is fraught with difficulties, it is also true that the discovery of an objective, real, and clearly binding legal principle involves great difficulty for the judge as well. The comparatively infrequent[11] cases where a delegate actually attempts to discover the existence and contour of the will of his constituency on the theory that such should guide his vote, even if against his will, must for our purposes be considered to be objective decision-making on the part of the legislator. This is so despite the fact that the substance of the decision will be clearly partisan. For isn't the judicial decision, in holding for one party over another, also partisan? Objectivity refers only to the decision-making *process*, not to the *substantive content* of the decision.

A systematic and rigorously empirical investigation might disclose the non-existence of the quantitative difference implied above between the number of objective decisions made by judges contrasted with legislators. This ought to be investigated. In other words, the number of judges who may be strongly precedent-oriented may not be any greater a proportion of judges than strict delegates are of legislators. Despite this possibility, it is the assumption herein that greater objectivity is built into the judicial decision-making process than into the legislative process. The reasons for this assumption are several other assumptions: (1) All appellate decision-makers accept the theory that the external objective binding force must be *consulted* in *all cases;* (2) *All* the position incumbents have been trained to think objectively in three years of rugged, heavily reinforced, professional school training programs and; (3) The decision is made under the most solemn and insulated of institutional circumstances designed to

---

[11] In the distribution of representative-role orientations (p. 281), only 14 per cent of the respondent legislators fell into the category of delegate— and the rather strict type noted above was undoubtedly only a small portion of this percentage.

promote objectivity. The writer believes the latter two factors are critical in distinguishing between the two processes under discussion—and between the judicial process and *all* other policy decision-making processes.

To recapitulate briefly, we have seen that the two major works discussed above which have explicated the concept of role have added something to our search for a useful specification of role. Nonetheless, we are far from our goal of finding and adapting one concept which can assist us in the confirmation of the principal proposition set out at the commencement of this chapter. There are just too many differences between that which has been studied and that which we want to study. At any rate, the previous discussion of role, legislative role, and judicial role has unquestionably clarified what we do *not* want in the way of precision and operations in the role concept acceptable for our purposes.

Furthermore, to the writer's knowledge, *no design to date has made an attempt to relate discovered and measured role variance to differences in decisional output*. In fact, the authors of *The Legislative System* make this latter point quite clear about the nature and scope of their study:

> An obviously important question for future research concerns the differences in behavior which follow from legislators' taking one or another of the representational roles in different legislative situations.[12]

Thus the work is cut out for us. One must work out a satisfactory operationalization of judicial role, and do this in the context of relating any variance in such (or the existence versus nonexistence of it) to a difference in decision (objective versus nonobjective or more or less objective).

The remainder of this chapter will emphasize this interrelationship of role with policy-making, specifically the judicial role with the judicial decision. It is beyond the scope of this chapter to attempt to reduce the notion of judicial role to any operational,

---

[12] *Ibid.,* p. 282.

i.e., measurable unit (either dichotomous 0 and −1; or scalable 0, +1, +2, +3, etc.). Rather, at this point, it seems more important to the development of our general scheme to recommend a general design for some potential research endeavors capable of testing our major hypotheses. By doing this, we will not only be making positive suggestions at a much greater level of specificity as to what is meant by judicial role, but will also be specifying the type of relationship we think is the major one involved in a theory of appellate judicial decision-making. For it must be recalled that a mere explication of judicial role is simply an exercise in description. As such, it is all too short a step in the development of any theory. We have had enough of this in traditional and contemporary political science. Thus far in this book, I have only attempted to explicate the *concept* we believe is nuclear to the conceptual scheme of the appellate process. Now I want to elaborate upon the type of interaction I believe is involved between all of the components of that process. This might be considered to be an explication of a theoretical or conceptual scheme. All this seems to be an acceptable clarification procedure prior to the endeavor to operationalize the concepts—key and subsidiary—in any working theory about the appellate judicial decision-making process. This latter exercise comprises the final portions of Chapter IV.

The research suggestions presented next cover as wide a field of possible social science techniques as appears available for the study of the critical relationships. I have attempted to select procedures from the real world, and from the social science laboratory; from the survey, and from the modern simulation technique; from direct methods, and the most indirect; from both macro and micro levels of analysis.

SOME PROPOSED STUDIES OF THE KEY PROPOSITION

Value and Limitation of Explication through the Macro Study: the Field Study

The major reason for designing a study at the macro level is demonstrably clear: It is at this level of study that one can validly confirm or disconfirm the hypotheses intact. This is so because we are dealing with the actual, life-sized phenomenon under study. Of course such a positive value has its costs, and these will be discussed.

Another way which the phenomenon I propose to study might be, and has occasionally been, described is as the particular relationship between two value systems of the appellate judge, i.e., judicial role values (precedent versus situation orientation) and the substantive attitudes (social, economic, and political) involved in given cases or sets of cases within a particular institutional context. Thus, we need at least two measurements, that is, two scales or two dichotomies.

A first step might be to find a series of appellate cases (state or federal) classifiable as political decisions. In order to maximize the objectivity of that concept, the decision of whether a case is political or not should be made by a panel of experts, e.g., political scientists, law professors, judges, etc., possibly through some type of sorting technique. This concept of political should not be confused with that amorphous, cloudy device employed upon occasion by the Supreme Court of the United States.[13] Political, here, is intended to mean a decision which relates to the notion of policy-making. Policy-making might be stipulated to include all legal decisions whose principles concern either a substantial segment of the existing population within the jurisdiction of the court (e.g., nation, state, circuit) or the distribution, boundaries, modifications, etc., of the powers, rights, duties, and privileges of governmental or public institutions. Cases such as *Youngstown Tube, Brown v. Board of Education,* and the recent New Jersey case which revoked the common-law privilege of non-responsibility in tort for charitable institutions,[14] would seem to fall comfortably within these definitions. The fuzziness of the words "substantial" and "comfortably" is conceded. Only near—

---

[13] We refer to the line of cases which extends roughly from such as *Colegrove* v. *Green* 328 U.S. 549 (1946) through *Baker* v. *Carr* 369 U.S. 186 (1962).

[14] *Callopy* v. *Newark Eye and Ear Infirmary* 27 N.J. 29 (1958).

if not total—unanimity of the experts would be acceptable in approaching an objective standard.

Our next step would be to discern precisely what social, political, or economic values were involved in these cases. Perhaps the same panel might be asked to extract such from the written opinions of the court. Or we might be able to employ content or factor analysis techniques (as in Kort, *et al.*[15]) to ascertain which relevant values were involved in the cases. Then we would have to construct, adapt, or adopt an item questionnaire which would measure how respondents stand on the various substantive values involved in the case or cases. After accomplishing this, we would select, probably at random, other judges or legal scholars from various parts of the country and administer this questionnaire in order to obtain a value portrait of each respondent. Next, we would present subjects with the facts of the same case (or cases) but which would be set forth as a moot situation, plus a short statement of the law of the fictitious jurisdiction (which would be the law involved in the actual cases), and ask them to decide the case and write a short opinion. Should we be fortunate enough to find that some of the respondents come to different decisions than the original court did, or used different lines of logic despite substantially similar substantive value scores, we would then compare the results obtained through a concurrent or subsequently administered second questionnaire.

The second questionnaire would concern the judicial role (or role values as related to thought process) of the appellate judicial decision-maker. Hopefully, the items that comprise it would be taken from a preliminary, open-ended type of questionnaire, or an interview on the nature of the judicial role as perceived by those considered to be role definers. Our hypothesis

---

[15] Fred Kort, "Predicting Supreme Court Decisions Mathematically: A Quantitative Analysis of the Right to Counsel Cases," *American Political Science Review*, 51 (1957), 1–12; "Content Analysis of Judicial Opinions and Rules of Law", Chapter 6 of *Judicial Decision-Making;* See also, Franklin M. Fisher, "On the Existence and Linearity of Perfect Predictors in 'Content Analysis', *MULL*, 60 (March, 1960), 1–9.

would be something along the lines of: The more importance the subject attached to such possible appellate judicial decision-making role factors as adherence to *stare decisis,* staying as close as possible to precedent, deductive logic, objectivity, or impartiality, or in Schientagean terms (since these are apparently some of his perceived role elements), thoroughness and open-mindedness, the greater the likelihood that the subject decision would *not* conform to a high score in the relevant substantive values believed by the experts to underlie the original decision. As a verification procedure we could ask the judges involved in the actual cases to respond to both substantive value and judicial role questionnaires.

Of course the troubles involved in inducing judges to respond to questionnaires on judicial role and substantive values would probably be infinitely greater than those encountered by Nagel in the relatively non-prying questionnaire which he distributed to judges. Undoubtedly the return of such questionnaires, particularly the ones dealing with political, economic and social values, would be a good deal less than the one-third reported by Nagel. The various problems involved in this scanty return are handled in Chapter V.

Another problem is that of the potentiality of this kind of study for disturbing the judicial process itself. This issue has many facets. However, our main purpose at this point is merely to suggest research which is *theoretically fruitful* and even remotely possible that, if we could conduct it, would greatly add to our knowledge about the appellate judicial decision-making process. Our aforementioned primary purpose is to explicate the concept of judicial role in interaction with other variables through a more concrete discussion of that which must be observed and how to go about observing it. Real difficulties may currently prohibit any actual study, but should not deter us from considering the kind of research which needs to be done in order to gain the desired knowledge.

Laboratory Study

If we cannot obtain the minimally necessary judicial cooperation (certainly the greatest likelihood at this time), perhaps we can resort to an increasingly fashionable social science laboratory technique which would keep us at the macro-level and be feasible as well as more parsimonious than the field study. We refer to the simulation experiment.[16] Law schools may be justifiably proud in pointing to the moot court procedure as a direct ancestor of the social science simulation. And indeed in this instance the simulation would be a moot court presentation. We however, unlike the law school's moot court exercise, would be interested in how the outcome was arrived at rather than the way the advocate presented the issue or the legal content of the decision *per se*. The Bevan *et al.* jury study at Emory University is probably the best as well as the most dramatic example of a type of simulation technique for studying some aspect of the domestic judicial decision-making process.[17] It has, though, very limited utility for those who worry along with the rule skeptics.

By the use of simulation, we could accomplish everything projected in the field macro study described above. We could recruit lawyers, law professors, and retired judges for our "courts" and ask them to respond to many questionnaires, including the types just discussed above, in order to test our hypotheses.

One major objection to this procedure is that these experiments would not have too high a validity quotient. All such findings are only minimally generalizable to the real world, and one of the major hypothetical reasons for this is that a real courtroom situation and a real case do not exist. This was also a major objection to the Bevan study, as well as to the Strodtbeck field jury study. In other words, because of the fact that everyone involved in such a study recognizes the artifice and experimental nature of the environment, they may behave differently than they would

---

[16] See the recent book edited by Harold Guetzkow, *Simulation in the Social Sciences* (Englewood Cliffs, N.J.: Prentice-Hall, 1962). In particular, see the introductory article by Richard E. Dawson on the general value and nature of the simulation experiment.

[17] William Bevan, et al., "Jury Behavior as a Function of the Prestige of the Foreman and the Nature of his Leadership," *Journal of Public Law*, 7 (1958), 419.

under the real conditions. However, there are available methods which can assist in maximizing the validity which is inherent in the simulation study situation.[18]

One way in which we may maximize the representativeness of the judges is to develop an index, formulated through analysis of the data gathered as discussed above, of judicial role elements and to select through the administration of similar questionnaires, the erstwhile judges, law school professors, and lawyers whose concept of the judicial role most conforms to the modal or average concept. This would most closely approximate the merger of the sophisticated legal mind with what could be considered typical judicial composure. Also, in order to further maximize the reality of the situation, steps might be taken to administer tests which would also discover the role-taking ability of the participants.[19] Those who scored high in ability to take a role would be preferred as subjects.

Nonetheless, whether through field research or laboratory simulations, if this type of hypothesis were substantially confirmed, we would be at the threshold of a whole series of studies designed to identify and measure those factors which might truly distinguish the common-law judge from the congressman, the federal communications commissioner, and the like. We might be at the beginning of devising a means to isolate and measure those factors which have brought about radical departures in behavior from what many (including the appointing President) expected from those appointed to the bench. The ostensible postappoint-

---

[18] For information on the Chicago work see Dale W. Broeder, "The University of Chicago Jury Project," *Nebraska Law Review*, 38 (1959), 744.

[19] Of course, the investigator must make a correction (implicitly) for the fact that the subject, in addition to responding to the task set for him, is also enacting the role of subject-in-an-experiment. Theodore R. Sarbin, "Role Theory," *Handbook of Social Psychology*. (Reading, Mass.: Addison-Wesley, 1954) I, 228. However, despite this problem, it would seem desirable to obtain some indication as to how well any given lawyer or law school instructor might take the role of the judge. In other words, we should either construct or adapt a measurement device to determine the degree of "as-if" skill that a potential respondent has. See pp. 236–38 of the Sarbin contribution cited above for discussion of some such devices and findings.

ment change in attitude of such as Hugo Black, Earl Warren, and Felix Frankfurter might well be ascribable to the juxtaposition of their various substantive attitudes against a new, perhaps more central or important, set of values, i.e., the judicial role. Perhaps the judicial role values were themselves theretofore simply latent. This suggestion is related to Grossman's point in Chapter I.

Micro Study

Objections to such macroscopic approaches to the study of the judicial decision-making process will include the arguments that they are highly naive, hardly feasible, and definitely not parsimonious. Undoubtedly the costs would be high; gaining the respondents' cooperation would be a major project in itself, and establishing a simulation situation would be fraught with serious pitfalls. These are certainly key problems to be considered. Since they are not solved as of now, and since their solution would take a great deal of time, energy, thought, and money, it seems only fair to present some more feasible and economical approaches which utilize the concept of judicial role as a key for the development of a theory which will lead to a more firm understanding of the judicial decision-making process. The writer believes, however, that the above-discussed uses of the concept of judicial role would maximize its utility in any study of that process.

We have already observed that there are not many studies of the other parts of the political system which utilize the concept of role. But as noted, there are *some* which do result in the accumulation of pertinent empirical data. In adapting any techniques employed in the study of these other sub-processes of the political system, e.g., the legislative process, we must be careful to avoid the type of mistake made by some analysts. But this is not a particularly difficult problem in dealing with the concept of role, particularly as we have explicated it. For instance the patent differences in the institutional context compels us to make necessary changes in the type of questions we should ask on a questionnaire. An advantage of the questionnaire as a social science technique is that it is flexible. A bloc analysis considers a vote to be a vote whether legislative or judicial. It is an analytic method which is incapable of adaptation and thus of little value in collecting data which will help us to understand any possible differences in process.

One particular study of the legislative process which seems to be readily adaptable to a study of the judicial process, and which promises to gather information pertinent to judicial role is a shorter one by the authors of *The Legislative System* which is found in a reader called *Introductory Readings in Political Behavior*.[20] It would be pointless here to discuss their specific findings; rather, it would seem sufficient to furnish some idea of the hypothesized results, namely that "legislators' conceptions of their role as legislators will be a crucial factor governing their legislative behavior."[21] This clearly establishes its relevance for us.

It could probably be stated with a high degree of certainty that judges, whether precedent- or situation-oriented, are influenced significantly by the arguments presented by lawyers in their briefs prior to oral argument. Particularly in certain types of public policy decisions, lawyers are currently prone to include a good deal more than simple listings and interpretations of decisions and statutes into their briefs, e.g., public interest arguments, social science data (charts, tables, etc.), and social science theory and interpretation of relevant data.[22] This raises several crucial questions for us. For instance, do all judges pay the same type or amount of attention to all materials? Are there different types of such materials in the eyes of different judges? Do some judges feel that some material is irrelevant, unimportant, and not to be considered? Do various judges give some types of material more or less credibility? And how do these answers relate to their conception of the judicial role? How do they relate to their orientation—and, in fact, can we not impute and measure their orientation, that is, role conception, through such questionnaires? Might this not be an interesting type of indirect measurement device? That is, a judge who says that he places great value on

---

[20] (Chicago: Rand McNally & Company, 1960).
[21] *Ibid.*, p. 389.
[22] The prototype of this is, of course, the famous "Brandeis Brief."

social science data and theory can be considered to be situation-oriented, while those who consider such to be irrelevant can probably be placed somewhere along the precedent-oriented side of the continuum. A further step, upon the derivation of the taxonomy of role orientations toward the social, as opposed to the legalistic, argument would be to observe the relationship between the judges' role portraits as described and measured through one of the other suggested methods. A high correlation might indicate that we have indeed discovered a good indirect measure of the appellate judicial decision-making role conception.

Among other factors to be observed would be the judges views on: (a) what type of data or data presentation in the oral argument is more worth listening to; (b) the influence of this information on the judges' own views of the nature of the social problem related to the litigation *sub judice;* (c) whether the judges believe that this information (or what information) affords valuable help in arriving at a decision; (d) whether the judge believes that this information affects the opinions or decisions of other judges (whom he believes to have similar or dissimilar role orientations). On the basis of all this information, it would then be interesting to turn toward the briefs and the ultimate disposition of the cases and see what relationships we could discover. Such a procedure, it is believed, would probably yield results of value in our endeavors to learn more of the judicial process and its intimate connection with the judicial role as thus far explicated.

Of course there is much more inference involved in this type of study of the value-role interaction hypothesis. The empirical referent is substantially separated from its concept (role).

If we could begin studies along all the three lines suggested above, then criticism of the way of judicial behavioralism could be much more specific and directed towards advancing our knowledge of the judicial process. At least we would be on the road toward a more precise benchmark of our ignorance.

SUMMARY

We have seen that, thus far, a wide hiatus exists between the theory and methods of the two major groups of analysts involved in the study of the judicial process. The width of this gap is rather surprising considering that both are essentially interested in describing the workings of the judicial psyche as the key to their general aims. The overlapping background shortcomings of the scholars in each of these two groups has probably led to the less than firm grasp of (a) a general theoretical orientation or framework for the subject matter, or (b) a plan for the necessary task of accumulating, assembling and interpreting relevant data.

We have observed that, contrary to what they implicitly promised, the political behavioralists for the most part have not directed their energies toward studying the peculiar intellectual motivational-institutional interactions that have traditionally been theorized as characterizing the appellate process. Their efforts, though systematic and rigorous, while they have led to more precise description of much that was already known to exist, have had no real explanatory insights into the hows and whys of these phenomena, that is, the pattern of judicial decisions. They have, by and large, avoided the essentials. As we have seen, their statistically-based propositions, though impressive in their descriptive precision and ostensible prediction potential, have several fundamental flaws.

Moreover, we have observed that the prominent legal scholars whose work we have surveyed have been far more comprehensive, and much more directly concerned with problems involved in the appellate process, but also far more vague, imprecise, and rambling. However, from all of the materials scanned, we did extract what appear to be several principle components in the judicial decision-making system, or, in other words, the key factors which must be involved in any working theory of judicial decision-making. All of these men cover the nature of the use of precedent in every case. The judicial role revolves about how and to what extent the rules of law are employed in relationship to many other current situational factors in order to arrive at a correct decision. In addition to this factor, another cardinal factor to identify and measure is that part (or parts) of the judge's complete value system which would predispose him to decide for one side or the other in each case before him. A third factor of great significance, but which this book has not yet treated in any detail, would seem to be the degree of clarity of control that a case or a series of cases seems to have in the immediate factual situation before the judge, whether he be precedent- or situation-oriented. Of course the fact that the issue is presented in a unique way and that it is to be stated in unique ways may also prove essential. An understanding of the nature of the interactions between these stated variables would be a giant step toward an understanding of the appellate process. However, one other major factor must also be considered, that is whether or not the interaction between judicial role, the judges' values and the existence of clear precedent will produce an objective, impartial, and just decision.

In discussing the work done on the concept of role, I attempted to point out some possible approaches toward a further delineation of the variables involved, and to give some suggestion about testing them under the most lifelike conditions. Results gained through these designs and techniques can be of great validity since the actual phenomena which we wished to understand would be the actual object of study. But as is perfectly obvious to everyone, such schemes are not feasible. Social science has a long way to go before it can penetrate even less sacred sancta than *supreme* courts. The simulation type of experiment or some quasi-experimental variation thereon would seem to be the feasible macro-oriented study available to us. It is here that ingenuity must be put to the test.

The next step is to devise some feasible way to isolate and test these three main variables in interaction and their impact upon the judicial decision in at least a reasonable facsimile of the appellate decision-making context. From the various kinds of any such tests, we will gain a capability to accumulate the relevant, empirical data from which we can alter and modify our hypotheses and eventually work towards a general theory of the judicial decision-making process—if, of course, the data demonstrates the likelihood of the existence of any such real and distinctive process.

Chapter IV

The Working Theory:
Approach, Hypotheses, and Operations

Playing the role of nihilist can furnish ample reward for the academician. Negativism, as well as skepticism, can be a joyous pastime. Each has its real value to any discipline, whether in the arts or sciences. But such a role is one for him who seeks the luxury of relative invulnerability, for being a critic is in many ways an easier lot than being creative in one's own thought. There is really much less to lose—and so much less chance to lose it. After all one is in a far more secure position when he attacks a notion or traditional mode and attempts to point out its flaws: its routine, its unexamined assumptions, and its logical inconsistencies. Tangible criteria of disproof exist, and the academic assailant can merrily wreak havoc with his victim's work. The field of the assailant's error is limited by that which his target has already set forth positively. He has, as it were, a limited responsibility. On the other hand, he who would undertake to present some notions of theory or to present a variation in the basic paraphernalia of research in any field, sets himself on the chopping block. One's *own* shortcomings and perhaps lack of scope will then stand out with startling clarity. Thus far in this book, the emphasis has quite strongly been that of criticism.

Another far less obvious route followed by academicians who avoid the necessity of exposing their academic necks is the construction of extremely high-level theories. Such theoretical structures can be contested, but they rarely can be disproved. A few who travel this road are avoiding the consequences of their own vulnerability. However, in disciplines which employ scientific standards of proof and verification, the questions are characteris· tically asked: *Precisely* what are you talking about? and *How* can you *prove* it? This has the effect of discouraging (though fortunately not totally eliminating) the practice of wild, high-level conceptualization in the sciences. Political science has had —and still has—more than its share of general theorists, philosophers, and students of both. But as political science continues to acknowledge more and more of its commitment to scientific method, those who would profess the utility and desirability of employing that approach need to adhere as closely as possible to the most rigorous requirements of that approach. Their need now is for theory, yes, but for operationally workable theory. As should be clear by now, that is the commitment of this writer.

The above two beliefs probably explain the goal of this study, which is the creation of a working theory closely related to some hard, empirical data. However, before I get to the content and composition of this working theory, one major step must be undertaken. After negating so many various techniques of study (scientific and otherwise), I believe it incumbent to *justify* my own general choice of *approach* and technique. Then progress can be made in developing a theoretical structure. First the conceptual and operational definitions of the major constructs in the analytic framework must be specified. Then some of the hypotheses derivable from that framework must be presented. After these steps are taken, the tools for a study must be developed, some data collected, and an analysis of the findings (with all appropriate warnings and qualifications) presented. But first things first.

DISCUSSION AND JUSTIFICATION OF THE APPROACH

Experimental Method

Chapter III alluded to some of the advantages and disadvantages of the experimental method. However, it is the view here that it is an important enough method if not *the* important method to be understood and appreciated if political science is going to make significant headway in its scientific endeavors. As H. J. Eysenck has stated:

> It must be admitted, of course, that experimentation in the motivational field is very much more complex and difficult than in almost any other, but, nevertheless, it may safely be surmised that until psychologists come to grips with the problem, much of their work will be of purely academic interest.[1]

Abraham Kaplan is a bit more flowery in his premise of experimentation as a tool for the advancement of the behavioral sciences. A few quotations from him will suffice. For instance:

> It is experimentation that expresses the basic empiricism of science. The scientist cannot lead us into nature's secret retreats unless he will risk having her slam the door in his face; experiment knocks on the door.

> Experiment is the consummation of the marriage of reason and experience, and though it is not in itself the life of the mind, it is the most passionate and fruitful expression of our intellectual life and loves.

> Experiment is the device by which we strip appearances from reality, and by putting matters to a test, distinguish dependent from independent variables.[2]

Kaplan is cautious enough to warn the true believer in experimentation against overestimating the value of such a technique. However, this warning is mainly directed to him who would claim that experimentation is the *only* way to knowledge.

Harold Lasswell, in discussing the past, present and future of the political science discipline—particularly in a policy science context, also warns of some of the problems regarding experi-

---

[1] H. J. Eysenck, *The Psychology of Politics* (New York: Frederick A. Praeger, 1955), p. 252.
[2] Abraham Kaplan, *The Conduct of Inquiry* (San Francisco: Chandler Publishing Company, 1964), 145–147.

mentation.[3] However he too points out its crucial value to any discipline which attempts to understand its phenomena scientifically. Lasswell emphasizes the limitations on experimentation which relate to the lack of credibility that its results will have in the eyes of policymakers, although he does point to certain limitations in the technique itself.

Nevertheless, despite its palpable value, experimentation has not been a widely borrowed technique in political science. Moreover, political scientists are apt to equate it exclusively with the simulation exercise. Experimentation, though, involves far more than that. Thus it will behoove us at this point to spend a bit of time on a discussion of the technique of experimentation. If it is a diversion, I believe that it is one worth the while.

Political scientists who emphasize the notion of science might stutter and stammer when the question is posed: How can you represent a science when you cannot put that which you study into a laboratory and experiment on it? There are many answers available to this query. These range from analogy (pointing out that neither can astronomers) to direct refutation (citing the efficacy of simulation techniques). Nevertheless the feeling is still strong that, come what may, political science can never really be an experimental science. This is substantially true, for much within its boundaries does not appear to be amenable to laboratory or natural laboratory manipulations. Yet this really evades the major question. For political science's main variables probably can be put into an *experimental frame of reference* and its manipulations can be of an indirect type, as in sociology and psychology.

Richard C. Snyder, in his essay "Experimental Techniques and Political Analysis: Some Reflections in the Context of Concern over Behavioral Approaches," has provided us with an excellent treatment of the entire scope of the problem.[4] After discuss-

---

[3] Harold D. Lasswell, *The Future of Political Science* (New York: Atherton Press, 1963).

[4] In James C. Charlesworth (ed.), *The Limits of Behavioralism in Political Science* (Philadelphia: The American Academy of Political and Social Science, 1962).

ing many of the issues whirling about use of the behavioral approach in political science, Professor Snyder presents six operating agreements. These six agreements, calculated to maximize the effectiveness and to limit the deleterious effects of the use of experimental techniques in the study of politics, are as follows:

(a) a broad conception of the science which includes preverification operations—"discovery" of variables, generation of hypotheses, tentative elimination of some competing hypotheses, construction of heuristic models or replicas of reality and so on;

(b) a strict adherence to the major concerns of the political scientist, that is, a focus on political institutions and processes, on the aggregates, groups and organizations which comprise and function within a governmental context, on relevant intergroup and interorganizational relations, and on the individual as a political actor (voter, decision-maker);

(c) a reliance on accumulated political wisdom, and on a literature containing propositions about political behavior held with varying degrees of confidence, as sources of variables and hypotheses;

(d) a primary objective of arriving at propositions and theories having a manifest political content;

(e) a recognition that experimental techniques are only supplementary—to be employed in a multiple strategy which includes field research (case studies, direct observations, surveys, and so forth) and propositional inventories;

(f) a loosening of the definition of "experiment" to include "quasi-experimental" design—those in which full control by the experimenter is lacking.[5]

The first two operating statements are agreed to unequivocally. In concurring with the third I must point out that the literature in the subject matter area of the judicial process is almost totally devoid of relevant propositions. Thus my experimental

---

[5] *Ibid.*, p. 101.

endeavor in this particular study will be almost completely *exploratory*. The fourth operating statement is also completely accepted. The fifth, however, relates to the review of the literature in Chapter I. Professor Snyder is by and large on sound theoretical grounds in stating that all should agree that experimental techniques ought to be only supplementary. An essential qualification which he omits, though, is that this prescription need not be adhered to when the other available techniques are either unfeasible or not parsimonious in a given area of study. In some cases—and I believe it to be the case in the area of judicial decision-making up to this moment—it might best be the primary technique and all others supplementary. F. Stuart Chapin has stated that

> When observation alone fails to disclose the factors that operate in a given problem, it is necessary for the scientist to resort to experiment.[6]

This might be akin to Kaplan's notion of the "heuristic experiment" or the "exploratory experiment."[7] I feel that this is the case for the study of the judicial process. This is because there is, by the nature of the process, too much that is unamenable to observation. The sixth statement is the most important practical notion of the series, that is, the one which recognizes the necessity for the quasi-experiment. Its importance stems from the fact that *it is the quasi-experiment with which I deal.* However, before quasi-experimentation can be carefully discussed, at least a brief glance must be taken at what is meant by true experimentation.

The usual way of defining experiment is to provide a very general definition. A good example of this is Chapin's:

> Experiment is simply observation under controlled conditions . . . The line between observation and experiment is not a sharp one. Observation tends gradually to take on the char-

---

[6] *Experimental Designs in Sociological Research* (New York: Harper and Brothers, 1947), p. 1.
[7] Kaplan, *op. cit.*, p. 149.

acter of an experiment. Experiment may be considered to have begun when there is actual interference with the conditions that determine the phenomenon under observation.

The fundamental rule of the experimental method is to vary only one condition at a time and to maintain all other conditions rigidly constant. There are two good reasons for this procedure: in the first place, if two conditions are varied at one time and an effect is produced, it is not possible to tell which condition is responsible, or whether both have acted jointly; in the second place, when no effect ensues, how can we tell which condition is responsible, or whether one has neutralized the other.[8]

Also, according to Arnold Rose:

An experiment consists simply of applying a stimulus to some object, holding constant the other possible stimuli or conditions which might affect the object simultaneously, and noting the changes that occur in the object, presumably because of the application of the stimulus. The purpose of the experiment, then, is to discover cause-and-effect relationships applicable to certain classes of objects.[9]

Thus the elements of condition and stimulus are always present and must be varied, manipulated, or controlled. The experimenter hypothesizes that a particular variation in a condition or stimulus which he has brought about will (or will not) affect the unit(s) he is observing to a certain degree or in a certain way. He must construct both observation and measurement devices to detect and measure any such change in the unit(s) of observation. If no change is perceived after the experimental treatment is administered, then the null hypothesis is confirmed. Any change, since all other conditions which might be conceived of as varying and possibly affecting the status of the unit(s) of observation have been removed as a varying factor (that is, they have been held constant), can only be attributed to the variation in the experimentally manipulated condition. A cause and effect

---

[8] Chapin, *op. cit.*, p. 1.
[9] *Theory and Method in the Social Sciences* (Minneapolis: University of Minnesota Press, 1954), p. 274.

relationship will have been confirmed and the degree or amount of change recorded. Thus one may have established a clean, empirical proposition which is subject to objective and precise verification or disverification through subsequent experimentation.

Professor Snyder's essay deals at some length with various attempts at experimentation in political science to date. As noted above, the list is quite short. Snyder, after giving his own definition of experiment, divides it into two kinds: the quasi-experiment and the artificial experimental situation. The latter type "involve[s] simulation, that is, the attempt to induce realistic effects and to reproduce properties of reality."[10] I have already discussed the advantages and disadvantages involved in employing a simulation technique to explore the relationships derivable in our conceptual scheme—and have decided, at least for now, to reject it for such purposes.

The Quasi-Experiment

The former type, the quasi-experiment, does offer some very interesting possibilities. The basic idea is not novel, only the label is somewhat unique. The idea is well presented in one of the major psychology research method books:

> Hypotheses about effects of attributes of individuals (rather than of the situation in which they are placed) often are not amenable to experimental investigation in the sense of manipulation of the "independent" variable by the investigator. To be sure, a hypothesis that hungry subjects will be more likely to interpret ambiguous pictures as representing food than will subjects who are not hungry can be tested experimentally; the degree of hunger can be controlled reasonably well by specifying the length of time subjects must go without eating before viewing the pictures. Many attributes of individuals, however, cannot be manipulated in this way. Non-manipulatable attributes are involved, for example, in such hypotheses as: brain damage impairs the ability to think abstractly; or, people will tend to remember those parts of a message that are consistent with their own views and to forget those that are contrary. The investigator working with human subjects will not manipulate the

---

[10] Snyder, *op. cit.*, Experimental Methods, p. 103.

variable of brain damage willfully by destroying portions of the brain; he must seek existing cases of brain damage. And he cannot assign certain views to certain individuals; they bring their views with them. *The investigator achieves the variation he wants, not by direct manipulation of the variable itself, but by selection of individuals in whom the variable is present or absent, strong or weak, etc. He presents brain damaged and non-damaged subjects with the same task; he asks individuals with different views to read the same passage, etc.*[11]

Snyder uses the label of quasi-experimental in much the same way as Campbell and Stanley.[12] A portion of their idea is included in his statement that the quasi-experiment:

. . . permit[s] some of the advantages of repeated observations under changing conditions in natural social settings without entailing the greater degree of control by the experimenter we associate with the laboratory.[13]

To illustrate this, Snyder refers to Professor Harold Gosnell's rather famous political study *Getting Out the Vote*.[14] However, the Gosnell study was far more a true experiment[15] than a quasi-experiment, even though it was a field rather than a laboratory manipulation. Controls were carefully developed and the manipulation was practiced directly by the experimenter on the experimental groups and omitted on the control groups. Through this method the experimenters found that their treatment of the experimental groups (the circulation of leaflets) brought about a significant behavioral change (a 9 per cent increase in voter registration over those who had not received the circulars). This

---

[11] Claire Selltiz, et al., *Research Methods in Social Relations*, rev. ed. (New York: Henry Holt and Company, 1959). pp. 90–91 (emphasis added).

[12] Snyder, *op. cit.*, Experimental Methods, p. 103.

[13] *Ibid.*, p. 102.

[14] *Getting Out the Vote* (Chicago: University of Chicago Press, 1927).

[15] Professor Campbell has stated that Gosnell's book is the only true experiment of which he is aware which has been conducted by a political scientist on political phenomena.

is the essence of the true experiment: The creation of the conditions and the groups, the manipulation, and the observation and measurement. It is not the idea of the laboratory *per se* that is crucial; the true experiment *can* be worked in natural social settings. Gosnell did it. According to Campbell and Stanley:

> There are many natural social settings in which the research person can introduce something like experimental design into his scheduling of data collection procedures (e.g., the *when* and *to whom* of measurement), even though he lacks the full control over the scheduling of experimental stimuli (the *when* and *to whom* of exposure and the ability to randomize exposures) which makes a true experiment possible. Collectively, such situations can be regarded as quasi-experimental designs.[16]

They explicitly recommend the quasi-experiment when "better designs are not feasible."[17]

However, merely to lead us to what is loosely called the quasi-experimental design is tantamount to the master when he has been asked by the apprentice, "How do I fix it?," leading the apprentice to the toolbox and telling him: "Pick up a tool." Campbell and Stanley are not so vague. They are cautious enough to establish many safeguards for the groping tyro and to set out the precise description and best uses for each tool they describe. Little would seem to be gained by rummaging through the entire chestful of Campbell-Stanley quasi-experimental designs. The reader who is interested in the full range of these designs is directed to their monograph. I wish only to describe the particular technique (quasi-experimental design) which seems most apt for probing the theoretical relationships involved in the major concepts discussed in Chapter III.

A Variation on the Institutional Cycle Design

Generally speaking, the theoretical scheme holds that judges,

---

[16] Campbell and Stanley, *op. cit.*, p. 204.
[17] *Ibid.*

as people with a particular outlook acquired through special training, think differently than other human beings while making a certain type of decision. I have spoken of this before as judicial role (that is, precedent orientation). Actually, one could speak of the training as being an independent variable, and the precedent orientation or judicial role as an intervening variable. This peculiar role probably has its taproots in the basic foundations of the legal process, i.e., the initial training of the lawyer. It has been my belief that this factor in conjunction with several others will produce different decisional results from a situation in which those same factors interact upon people who do not have such a role conception. Thus, one is dealing with behavior believed to vary as a function of one certain natural conditioning factor induced at a prior time. A natural experimental manipulation exists: A few people go through law training; most do not. Can this training process and its possible impact upon the minds of the recipients be ignored? Campbell and Stanley, in discussing the institutional cycle design, were likewise interested in seeing the effect of prolonged institutional training (military) upon the minds of those (cadets) who were exposed to it. As they state:

> The fact that the experimental variable was recurrent and was continually being presented to a new group of respondents, made possible some degree of experimental control.[18]

Therefore, we are presented with the natural social manipulation which fits well within the entire theoretical orientation.

At this point, then, I hope that I have sufficiently justified the selected approach as *an* approach. In the next sections my aim is to set out more explicitly *what* is to be studied and how I intend to go about studying it. This will necessitate several steps: a precise set of conceptual definitions; the operations for the key ones; and the presentation of the main hypotheses derivable from the conceptual web. This done, the working theory will have been presented in full.

---

[18] *Ibid.*, p. 228.

MECHANICS OF THE STUDY

Definitions

Appellate Judge: the decision-maker in the appellate litigational context.

Appellate litigational context: a decision-making situation where each of two parties presents a dispute on appeal to a decision-maker for decision in his favor, making reference to the existence of legal precedent as containing principles which would constrain the judge to decide in his favor.

Clear legal precedent: legal precedent which has reached a point where it furnishes explicit guidelines as to which party in a dispute presented in the appellate litigational context ought to prevail.

Judicial role: the expected behavior of the judge characterized as being precedent-oriented, i.e., in an objective decision by referring to established legal precedent as the grounds for such a decision.

Legal precedent: a constitution, statute (legislation), or case law of the Supreme Court of the United States or the highest court of the jurisdiction in which the court is sitting.

Objectivity and objective decision: when a decision is actually based upon general principles, or when a decision differs, or the degree to which a decision differs, from that decision or those decisions which would have been reached by the decision-maker had he rationally decided in accordance with his own personal substantive value preferences.

Precedent orientation: the belief of an appellate judge that his decision in an appellate litigational context should directly relate to, be constrained by and be justified by, or be derivable from the established relevant, clear legal precedent.

Substantive value preference: that personal value or attitude or those values or attitudes of the appellate judge which are related to the particular social, economic, or political relationships which are the subject of the litigation and which result in a personal tendency to decide for one of the parties presenting his case for decision in the litigational context.

General Hypothesis

Once a legal precedent reaches a point of being clearly controlling in a dispute presented in an appellate litigational context, it will inhibit a substantive value preference of the decision-maker who assumes the judicial role, thus resulting in an objective decision.

Specific Hypotheses

1. If there is strong substantive value preference, clear legal precedent, and a precedent orientation, then the decision-maker in an appellate litigational context will tend to decide objectively.

2. If there is strong substantive value preference, ambiguous legal precedent, and a precedent orientation, then the decision-maker in an appellate litigational context will tend to decide in accordance with his own substantive value preference.

3. If there is strong substantive value preference, clear legal precedent, and no precedent orientation (a situational orientation), then the decision-maker in an appellate litigational context will tend to decide in accordance with his own substantive value preference.

4. If there is strong substantive value preference, ambiguous legal precedent, and no precedent orientation (a situational orientation), then the decision-maker in an appellate litigational context will tend to decide in accordance with his own substantive value preference.

5. If there is weak substantive value preference, clear legal precedent, and a precedent orientation, the decision-maker in an appellate litigational context will tend to decide objectively.

6. If there is weak substantive value preference, ambiguous legal precedent, and a precedent orientation, then the decision-

maker in an appellate litigational context will tend to decide in accordance with his own substantive value preference.

7. If there is weak substantive value preference, clear legal precedent, and no precedent orientation (a situational orientation), then the decision-maker in an appellate litigational context will tend to decide in accordance with his own substantive value preference.

8. If there is weak substantive value preference, ambiguous legal precedent, and no precedent orientation (a situational orientation), then the decision-maker in appellate litigational context will tend to decide in accordance with his own substantive value preference.

OPERATIONS FOR THE KEY CONCEPTS

Appellate Litigational Context

The appellate litigational context of which I speak is that of a court case, a dispute submitted for judicial decision. I am primarily interested in one phase of the judicial decision-making process, the appellate level. Thus in order to study the possible objectivity of the appellate decision, it is essential to present to all of our respondents (subjects) a case on appeal which must be decided by them. All of the respondents must be afforded equal opportunity to assume the position of appellate judge. Whether or not anyone will assume the judicial role as an incumbent of that position remains to be seen.

It would be highly unfeasible and expensive to set up a mock courtroom situation and argue a full case. This holds particularly true when laymen are involved in the exercise, as they are in this study. Thus to simplify the task and to gain feasibility and parsimony (within our own budgetary limits), I have settled on the device of presenting hypothetical cases (facts, plus the extant, relevant precedent) to all of the people involved in our quasi-experiment, using a questionnaire-type form. By explaining, on this questionnaire and through oral reinforcement of the written instructions, that they (the respondents) are to decide the case as a good judge should and give reasons for such a decision, the general outline of the appellate litigational context in which any appellate judge decides will have been created: He is a judge; there is a case on appeal which confronts him for decision; he is informed as to what the relevant legal precedent is; he is to present, in writing, for scrutiny, the reasoning upon which he bases his decision.

Obviously this is not exactly the same situation or context in which the judge decides. However, its failures as such are in some ways *less* conducive to bringing about objectivity than they are biased in favor of it. After all, the judge's decision is made in the collegiate and somber atmosphere of the institutional trappings and tradition of the real appellate situation. Thus, if a finding of significant objectivity should be obtained (the null hypothesis not confirmed) in our study, it would seem to augur well for finding a similar result in the real world.

The choice of any particular factual situations and relevant law which comprise the case situation will be, for the most part, an arbitrary one. The only criteria which would seem justifiable as limitations on selection are: (1) there should be a policy flavor involved in the case; (2) there should be different substantive areas in different cases so as to preclude similar substance as a systematic bias; (3) the issues raised ought to be ones on which people would have opinions and be willing to express them; (4) any issue on appeal should be a matter of law and not of fact; (5) the issues ought to vary in the intensity to which people will hold opinions on them so that the findings would be amenable to generalization about other than just hot issues.

Law Training Factor

Judges before they become judges are invariably lawyers. And lawyers before they are lawyers must go through the rigors of legal training in a law school. Law school, to describe it for those who have not had that experience, is a dreadfully difficult and tedious process (particularly in the first year). It is in this environment of extremely great tension and pressure that the legal mind is forged. Theoretically, fresh and keen minds are molded from the nonlegal thinker into the legal thinker through the law school process. The legal thinker (theoretically) is he who is a dispassionate seeker into the law, determined to find out whether any law is controlling in the litigation in which he is involved, and, if such law is found, to abide by it. Non-lawyers could never understand this process; this nagging belief that the law may well furnish the answer or very compelling guidelines which will dispose of the case correctly and justly. This is a main part of what was termed precedent orientation, and it composes what is believed to be the essence of what is usually considered to be the heart of the judicial decision-making role as opposed to any other decision-making role as it becomes manifest in the judicial decision. For purposes of the present exploratory and working theory, it is considered to be the pivotal factor.

As noted above, the treatment which induces this role posture does not have to be created and applied. Rather, in classic quasi-experimental style, one needs only to go into the real world and find those who have received the experimental treatment and those who have not. The former will be the experimental group, the latter will comprise the control group. The operation, for immediate purposes, is this simple dichotomy. A law school is defined simply as an institution of higher learning accredited by the American Association of Law Schools to award an LLB degree to those who have successfully completed at least a three-year curriculum. Those who have been through at least one and preferably two or more years of law school will be considered to have become sufficiently inducted into the process of legal thinking.

Substantive Value Preference (SVP)

In order to determine whether or not acceptance of law-school-wrought precedent-orientation by one assuming the judicial role does in fact significantly neutralize his own personal predisposition for decision based upon his own attitudes and values, one must also obtain accurate knowledge about the individual substantive value systems involved in any cases to be decided. We need to learn what they are and how intensely they are held by all of the respondents in both experimental and control groups.

The first step towards isolating this variable is the development of a device by which the direction of the predisposition in the relevant areas of the hypothetical litigation can be discovered. In other words, one must be able to discern with great precision *how the respondent would want to see each specific case decided if he had the power to make the law.* In the abstract, it seems that either open-ended (unrestricted) questions or structured (closed) questions are both capable of eliciting this data. Generally speaking, each type of question offers distinct advantages and disadvantages. The major difficulty in the open-ended question involves coding problems which lead to substantial unreliability of results. Two general difficulties in the structured or closed-ended question are the problems of phrasing the questions clearly and the distinct possibility that the experimenter may be putting words in the respondent's mouth.

In the course of several pilot studies, a number of other problems became apparent. I found, in exclusive use of the open-ended technique, that I could not detect with any confidence whatsoever which way a respondent was predisposed. For instance, in a hypothetical case which dealt with a state statute regulating apartment houses, tenement buildings, hotels, motels and similar places of lodging, I attempted to discover predisposition by an open-ended question phrased as follows: What are your *personal* views on state control of rent? Two of the many answers I found impossible to code were:

> I do however feel this is an excellent idea for the rentee but not for the rentor. This because a rentee could find an apartment which had been assessed low but because of improvement could demand higher rent. But also if the rentor couldn't benefit by improvement, i.e., higher rents, he would have no reasons to improve his property.

> I think that it [control of rent] is not a function of the state and should not be until such a time when it became impossible to rent property at a reasonable and fair price.

Answers like this made poor guidelines for determining whether or not the respondent would be sympathetic to the landlord or the tenant in the given factual situation. (Appendix A-1)

Most of the responses, however, did seem to be clear enough. For instance, there would appear to be little room to misinterpret predisposition in such responses to this question as:

Bah!
Opposed—constitutes a distortion of economic resources.
I see no need for state control of rent.

Unfortunately, a later pilot study developed to test rater-reliability in the prediction of respondents' predispositions, *viz.*, the specific case situations, demonstrated that even the apparently clear response to the open-ended question afforded predictability scarcely better than chance. There is a high correlation, it appears, between the generality of the questions and answers and the unpredictability of predispositions toward very specific factual circumstances. The situation confronting us is not unlike the problem a psychologist might have in furnishing a manufacturer with information on the manufacturer's employees' attitudes towards the company. Should the psychologist use the SRA Employer Inventory?[19] According to Anna Anastasi:

In the more carefully conducted employee attitude surveys, it is customary to construct special instruments for use in a given company. It is thus possible to tailor each question to local conditions and to obtain reactions to more specific characteristics of the particular job situation.[20]

Where there is a very specific set of circumstances to which one needs to apply the attitude, the greater the generality of the attitude, the less likely it is to cover the peculiar situation in which one is interested. Many confounding and confusing variables are bound to exist.

---

[19] Science Research Associates Mechanical Aptitude Test. It is intended to measure mechanical knowledge, space relations and shop arithmetic.

[20] Ann Anastasi, *Psychological Testing* (New York: The Macmillan Company, 1954), p. 579.

Subsequent attempts to refine the questionnaire by using simple structural Yes-No box questions led to similar disaster. Thus, as I am a good Aristotelian, my bipolar failure led me to the eventual use of a hybrid type device which did prove to be best. The solution was to start off with the open-ended query, then to employ several much more specific questions, and finally to end with a direct question or questions closely related in detail to the factual situation of the hypothetical case. For an abortion case situation developed through the pilot work, (Appendix A-2) the most specific, directly relevant questions were:

3. Might (abortion) be justified in order to safeguard the physical as well as the mental health of the mother? Only the physical? Only the mental?

4. Would your answer to question 3 remain the same if it were only probable (rather than certain) that the physical or mental health of the mother would be put in jeopardy by the birth process?

One reason for not using merely the single specific question which would include all the main, relevant facts in the subsequent case situation was an attempt to at least partially disguise the purpose of the attitude questionnaire. It was hoped that the essays written by the respondents on the open-ended part of the questionnaire would accomplish two major purposes. First, it was believed that this writing would take up much time and bring in enough other parts of other attitude universes so that what was happening would not be as obvious to the respondent when he finally got to deciding the cases which followed. Second, it was hoped that it could be a reserve to help the raters arrive at a correct prediction of a respondent's predispositions. According to the raters, it did serve this purpose well on many occasions.

In order to make certain that the rating of predisposition was accurate and objective in relationship to the specific factual situations of our hypothetical cases, a questionnaire consisting of two main parts was developed. There was (1) the attitude questionnaire discussed above (The substantive value preference questionnaires on the abortion and hospital cases are attached as Appendix B-1 and B-2), and (2) a presentation of only the factual segment of our hypothetical cases (that part of the hospital case which was considered to be the factual segment is indicated in Appendix A-3 and A-4 by brackets). The respondents were asked to express their opinions in the first part and then were asked to play the role of *legislator* in the second part by checking an appropriate box as to *how they would want the law to be* in each particular factual situation. They were to indicate how the law should *favor* one party or another. (Appendix C)

In order to maximize objectivity in coding the direction of the individual respondent's predispositions, a panel of experts was set up. This panel consisted of four men holding PhD degrees (two political scientists, one economist, and one psychologist. A short biography of panel members is attached as Appendix D.) Each panelist read the substantive value preference statements of the respondents and, keeping in mind the nature of the facts which would subsequently be presented to the respondent via the questionnaire, rated the predisposition of each respondent to favor one party or the other for each case. (A facsimile of the raters' sheets is attached as Appendix E.)

The panel achieved almost 80 per cent agreement in rating respondents' dispositions. When this unanimity existed among them, the accuracy of their prediction as to whether or not the respondent would want to see law favor one party or another in the subsequent fact situations was at least 90 per cent. In other words, when all four experts agreed that on the basis of the questionnaire responses they would predict that the respondent would want to see the law hold for either the plaintiff or defendant, their prediction was accurate over 90 per cent of the time. On the abortion case (*State* v. *Claire*), the raters, when in 4–0 accord, were 100 per cent correct. An inter-rater 3–1 agreement resulted in a range of accuracy from only 60 per cent to 85 per cent, depending upon the case. Thus, in order to eliminate much of the chance which could be involved in this variable, we decided to use only those respondents upon whom the panel unanimously agreed as to their predisposition.

Thus far in this section, I have discussed some operations involved in obtaining accuracy and objectivity in the factor of *direction* of substantive value preferences. Another problem which had to be faced was the arrangement of a method which would indicate the variation in *intensity* with which the respondents held their respective value preferences.

Although it would probably be possible to develop an intersubjective rating scheme in order to measure the intensity with which each of the values is held by each respondent, this seemed unnecessary. A simple, objective, and probably more accurate calibration device commonly used is one which asks the respondents themselves to rate their own intensity of feeling. This was easily accomplished by placing the following type of question at the bottom of each substantive value preference question page and requesting the respondents to check the appropriate response.

How strongly do you feel about this.
1. Extremely strongly   —
2. Very strongly   —
3. Strongly   —
4. Not strongly at all   —

This method is one which has been highly successful in social scientific research. According to Selltiz, *et al.*:

A graded series of response possibilities frequently gives the investigator additional or more accurate information than a dichotomous response and presents the question more adequately and acceptably to the respondent. The most common multiple-choice responses utilize three, four or five gradations, but larger numbers are sometimes appropriate. A widely used special form of multiple choice (the so-called 'cafeteria' question) asks the respondent to choose from a list of assorted words or statements one or more that best represent his own view. The items may or may not be arranged in order from high to low, good to bad, favorable to unfavorable.[21]

From their list of examples, a slight abridgement of the following was selected:

---

[21] Selltiz, *op. cit.*, pp. 568–69.

___ not strong at all
___ not very strong
___ rather strong
___ very strong
___ extremely strong[22]

There seemed to be little enough difference between "not very strong" and "rather strong" to eliminate one. The former was chosen.

These appear to be adequate operations for accurately determining the direction of the substantive value preferences of the respondents as well as the degree of intensity to which they hold these value positions.

Clarity of Legal Precedent

"The precedent is clear in this case," "The case-law states in no uncertain terms that. . . . ," "The case of *Skoloff* v. *Topf* leaves us no alternative but to decide. . . ." These are familiar phrases sprinkled liberally throughout common-law, statutory interpretation and constitutional law literature. In the terms used above these are also stating that there is clear legal precedent which ought to dictate (or furnish strong guidelines for) the direction of decision in the immediate factual dispute before the judge (he who has assumed the judicial role). It theoretically leaves him little to no choice in decision, despite the fact that his own values might lead him to decide otherwise. But obviously unless the case is, as lawyers say, "on all fours," there is always— to varying degrees—a difference in clarity. Since "all fours" cases are about as rare as bald sopranos, differences in degree of clarity of our cases had to be measured or at least dichotomized for our purposes. There has to be sufficient clarity in order for precedent orientation to spring into active use. One must be able to state at some point that a clarity is present, and that at another point an ambiguity arises. Both of these ought to be scalable.

---

[22] *Ibid.*

The problem of how to go about developing hypothetical cases in which the precedent is very clear and cases in which the precedent is very cloudy seems open to various solutions. Once again the panel of experts was used. Experts, in this situation, were thought to be people who professionally work with legal precedent. But unfeasibility once again reared its ugly head. Of the three main groups of scholars of legal precedent who would seem most likely to fit under the rubric of expert, only one group would seem to be readily accessible for this sort of project. Law professors, in lieu of judges and lawyers (particularly appellate advocates), probably believe they have the most time and probably do have the greatest inclination to participate in the type of rating exercise which would be necessary. Upon these assumptions, I turned to the law schools.

The procedure adhered to was as follows:

1. Through personal contacts, several law professors who reputedly had an interest in the social science approach to various problems of the judicial process were approached and persuaded to join the panel. The four who comprised the final panel did not need much persuading, however. All were eager to help, and they performed their task quickly and efficiently. All contributed toward ironing out some of the more glaring deficiencies in the hypothetical cases (Appendix F contains a short biographical sketch of each member of this panel.)

2. Each professor was approached separately and in person. They were asked to work separately and they did so. Thus independent but co-ordinated opinions were received which are in accord as to the distinct difference in the clarity-ambiguity character of each of the case situations presented to the respondents. Each professor was given a rating sheet which instructed him to circle a number from 0 to 3 next to a letter which represented each hypothetical case he was to read. Zero stood for "highly ambiguous," which was defined as "precedent is no guide to deciding for either party," while the 3 (the other extreme) stood for "perfectly clear." This was defined as: "the precedent leaves no doubt as for whom the court must decide." (A replica of the rating sheet is affixed as Appendix G.)

3. The idea of working out agreement between the experts on the panel through the mails was quickly discarded. Of the several law professors with whom some negotiation was transacted by mail, some did not answer at all and the few that did either misjudged the nature of their task or were "in haste" (as one law professor stated in his closing). Thus, the panel really became a panel, and the writer its moderator. It became necessary to make several trips back and forth to the individual members of the panel to hammer out the eventual agreement between them on all the cases.

Only one of the four experts on the final panel made the 3 and 0 choices throughout the original four sets of hypothetical cases. The others, through their rating sheet circles, personal statements, and conversation indicated that they felt a bit too constrained by the word "perfectly." However, as they now stand, the four experts are unanimous in their opinion that there is at least a two-point difference between the cases rated as clear and as ambiguous. That is the ambiguous cases were approximately between the 0 and the 1, while the clear ones were between the 2 and the 3. This is so in the hospital cases which are used for analysis in the next chapter. Their conceptualization preference is as "clear" and "not clear" rather than "perfectly clear" and "perfectly ambiguous." Again, for the immediate purposes of testing the hypotheses this would seem to be sufficient.

Objectivity of Decision

The conceptual definition of an objective decision includes decisions which are in accord with the decision-maker's substantive value preferences *if* that decision has been derived from a general principle. However, it is clear that it would be impossible to identify such decisions within the confines of the experimental situation. In other words, this would necessitate being able to discern the difference between a reasoning process and a rationalization process in the questionnaire answer. This is quite a risky business. One can only be certain that a decision is objective when it is in opposition to the coded substantive value preference of the respondent decision-maker. Thus objective decisions are those decisions which are opposed to the rated substantive value preference.

SUMMARY

The operationalization of these key concepts completes the development of the working theory. With this done and with the hypotheses ready for testing, a limited study was undertaken. The next chapter discusses a few details of the study procedure, some findings, and an analysis of those findings.

Chapter V

The Experiment:
Illustrations of Applicable Analytic Techniques

THE EXPERIMENT AND THE FINDINGS

The scope of the study which would have to be undertaken to arrive at any valid generalizations about the main hypotheses is enormous. Indeed the sampling problems which are inherent in this study would necessitate much financial assistance even to establish the nature of the populations with which one would have to deal. If the goal in this work were to prove or disprove systematically the major and minor hypotheses set out in Chapter IV, one would have had to solicit varied types of support over an extended period of time. However, as was stated several times, the goal of this study is chiefly heuristic. Insofar as the findings themselves are concerned, this study is exploratory rather than probative. Thus, in a sense, what has been conducted is a pilot effort calculated to observe the parts of a working model in interaction and to illustrate the usage of some quantitative and qualitative techniques which are capable of adequately testing the hypotheses against this data.

It was noted before that Kaplan has used the phrases "heuristic experiment" and "exploratory experiment."[1] In any sense of those words, that is precisely what is being done here. It is

---

[1] Kaplan, *op. cit.*, p. 149. (See note 6, Ch. IV).

easy for the philosopher of science to say that scientifically oriented researchers often couch poor experimentation under the labels "heuristic" and "pilot study." However, it isn't too easy for the researcher to develop good or sophisticated experimental techniques in the beginning of his exploration of a field. Harold Guetzkow exhorts his students to dirty their hands in the data. Such advice might as well apply to the philosopher observing the researcher.

Administrative Details

The questionnaires which supplied the data which are the subject of the subsequent analyses were administered from June through September, 1963. The control group (nonlaw students) consisted of undergraduate students in political science courses at Wayne State University. Approximately one hundred students participated. A like number of students were drawn primarily from Wayne State University Law School's senior class. The remainder were students from the law schools at The University of Michigan, Northwestern University, and Washington University of St. Louis.

Obtaining access to the law students who eventually participated and to their classroom time was far more difficult than gaining access to the undergraduates. Law professors, it seems, have a different set of values and a different view of their professional role than do liberal arts professors. Although the questionnaire was not allowed to be administered during class time in any but one law school class, many law students were persuaded by their professor to volunteer their time immediately following a class. They stayed in their class group. Thus, the classroom situation was held constant for both the undergraduate and law student groups.

All in all, the questionnaires took about 35 minutes to complete. The front page briefly introduced the respondent to the project (Appendix H). Then came the substantive value preferences questionnaire. Following that, the respondent came to what might be termed the appellate judge position page (Appendix I). The statement therein which reads that the respondent should decide the subsequent cases (there were four) "as you believe a good judge should decide it," was meant to be as ambiguous as it is. It was believed that differing role orientations would lead to differing perceptions of the word "good." The final stage was that of the hypothetical cases which the judges were to decide.

Before each session, the students involved were told by their professor and by the author of the great importance of this study. A relationship of this study to Northwestern's Law School was especially emphasized in order to solicit the law students' utmost cooperation.

Choice of Cases and Techniques

The course of the study disclosed several major problems. But rather than spend time in discussing what pitfalls to avoid in the type of research undertaken here, it will be sufficient to confine the presentation of findings to a two-case analysis. It must be clearly emphasized, however, that I have not selected the two cases (out of the original eight) which tend to confirm the hypotheses. Quite the contrary, others furnished far more impressive evidence for such a cause. Rather, the choice of the particular two cases was based solely upon criteria of reliability and validity. In other words, these cases are the soundest. This case analysis, then, is presented chiefly for representing the kinds of statistical and qualitative analyses which can be employed using the data collected by the research device constructed to test the hypotheses presented in Chapter IV. The conclusions are obviously tentative, although it might be added (particularly with the knowledge of what the other cases seemed to reveal), suggestive of future confirmation of some of the hypotheses.

The cases selected for analysis are the two hospital cases (Appendices A-3 and A-4) *Charney* v. *St. Mary's Mercy Hospital* and *Arthur* v. *St. Mary's Mercy Hospital*. The Charney case was one which was rated as "clear" by the experts, and the Arthur case was deemed "ambiguous" by them. No single respondent decided both of these cases—each decided three of the other hypothetical cases. In each set of four cases confronting each respondent, there were two clear and two ambiguous cases. Measures were also taken to mix up the sequence of clear-ambiguous cases as well as the sequence of content of the cases, i.e., hospital, rent control, abortion, etc.

The rating procedure on the questionnaire indicating predisposition-toward-charitable-institutions (Appendix B-2), given to approximately 100 undergraduate and 100 law students, yielded 77 of the former and 87 of the latter upon which all four raters agreed as to direction of decisional predisposition. Thus, the total N of this analysis is 164.

Specifically, as to technique, chi-square analyses (two-, three-, and four-dimensional) and analysis of variance would seem to be useful to test for any interactions of the main variables.[2] Moreover, some type of content analysis of the reasons employed by the law students (precedent-oriented) and the nonlaw students (situation-oriented) could probably be invaluable in understanding any differences in decision-making. All of this, it must be remembered, is in pursuit of the attempt to see whether or not the data can be taken to demonstrate that there is more objective decision-making and judicial role-playing on the part of the experimentally treated group (the law students), and if so, whether this occurs only or more so under one or two stated circumstances (existence of clear precedent, or relevant values held weakly).

More specifically, the interactions under scrutiny are those of three independent (or interdependent) factors upon one dependent variable. The hypotheses involve the interaction of substantive value predisposition, clarity of precedent, and role orientation of each respondent, and whether or not there is a noticeable and significant impact of any interaction among these factors upon the bringing about of objective decision-making (the dependent variable). Statistical techniques which can inform us which, if any, two-way or three-way interactions are

---

[2] For use of chi-square in more than two dimensions, see B. J. Winer, *Statistical Principles in Experimental Design* (New York: McGraw-Hill Book Company, 1962), pp. 629–632.

bringing about any significant proportion of objective decisions are employed.

Some objection might be raised as to the use of the chi-square technique with the occasionally sparse data available to this study. In discussing restrictions on the use of chi-square, Underwood, and others, have stated that "no theoretical frequency [expected or independence value per cell] should be smaller than 10."[3] This, however, is the conservative position. According to Edwards, it is generally agreed that the estimated frequency ought not to be less than 5.[4] But it is the opinion of some highly respected statisticians that even this might make little difference. Edwards notes:

> Snedecor, however, has recently said: "Accumulating evidence indicates that the inaccuracies which may be introduced by small expected numbers are not so serious as was formerly thought."[5]

This technique is justified in this specific instance, despite general misgivings, simply because of the nature of this specific study. After all I am simply analyzing the data in order to see whether it *indicates* that the hypothesized interactions are occurring.

The chi-square score of 7.20 with 11 degrees of freedom is not at all significant (Table 1). However, partition of the X^2 among the possible interactions indicated that some were worth further investigation, i.e.,: (1) the two-way interaction between law/nonlaw respondents and whether their decisions were in accord with or opposed to their substantive value predisposition (Interaction 4, Table 2); (2) the three-way interaction between law/nonlaw respondents, weak/strong value preference situa-

---

[3] Benton J. Underwood, et al., *Elementary Statistics* (New York: Appleton-Century-Crofts, 1954), p. 207.

[4] Allen L. Edwards, *Statistical Methods for the Behavioral Sciences* (New York: Rinehart and Company, 1954), p. 384.

[5] Allen F. Edwards, *Statistical Analysis* (New York: Rinehart and Company, 1946), p. 253.

TABLE 1

Significance of Interactions Among Three Main Variables as a Source of Influence Upon Objective Decision-Making: Four-Dimensional Chi-Square Analysis

	Law Students (LS)				Nonlaw Students (NLS)	
	Clear (CL)	Ambiguous (AMB)			Clear	Ambiguous
OPP Weak (WK)	9.2 *14*	8.0 *10*		OPP	8.2 *4*	7.1 *7*
ACC	17.8 *13*	15.4 *13*		ACC	15.8 *19*	13.6 *15*

	Clear	Ambiguous			Clear	Ambiguous
OPP Strong (ST)	6.7 *8*	5.8 *3*		OPP	5.9 *6*	5.1 *4*
ACC	12.9 *14*	11.2 *12*		ACC	11.4 *10*	9.9 *12*

$X^2 = 7.20$ $p < .70$ (non-sig.) d.f. $= 11$

(Numbers at top left of each cell are the expected frequencies of the cell. Numbers in italics are the observed frequencies.)

Key:

Orientation	LS — Precedent Oriented; law students
	NLS — Situation Oriented; nonlaw students
Nature of Decision	OPP — Decision opposed to substantive value predisposition ("objective" decision)
	ACC — Decision in accord with substantive value predisposition (subjective decision)
Clarity of Precedent	CL — Clear precedent case (*Charney*)
	AMB — Ambiguous precedent case (*Arthur*)

Strength of Predisposition   ST — Strongly held substantive value predisposition (3 or 4 box checked)

WK — Weakly held substantive value predisposition (1 or 2 box checked)

Illustration: The box (left, lower) stands for the following: The people therein are law students (LS) who held strong values (ST) on the issue of charitable immunity. Eight of them decided objectively (OPP)— (against their own values, and in the direction prescribed by the clear precedent (CL)). Fourteen of them followed their predisposition despite a contrary prescription of the precedent. On the right hand side of the box we see that only three of fifteen law students decided against their values. This side of the box (the AMB side) is comprised of those law students who decided the Arthur case, in which there was no precedent extant to guide in any particular decisional direction.

TABLE 2

Partition of X^2 in 4-Dimensional Table

Interaction	X^2	$p<$	d.f.
1. Total	7.20	.70	11
2. LS/NLS × WK/ST	0.00	1.00	1
3. LS/NLS × CL/AMB	0.32	.70	1
4. LS/NLS × OPP/ACC	2.51	.20	1
5. WK/ST × CL/AMB	0.03	.90	1
6. WK/ST × OPP/ACC	0.50	.50	1
7. CL/AMB × OPP/ACC	0.25	.70	1
8. LS/NLS × WK/ST × CL/AMB	0.07	.80	1
9. LS/NLS × WK/ST × OPP/ACC	2.31	.20	1
10. LS/NLS × CL/AMB × OPP/ACC	0.68	.50	1
11. WK/ST × CL/AMB × OPP/ACC	0.81	.50	1
12. LS/NLS × WK/ST × CL/AMB × OPP/ACC	—0.28*	.20	1

*Partitioning of X^2 may lead to a negative residual, which is an uninterpretable artifact. The 4-way interaction may be treated as negligible.

tions, and whether the decisions were in accord with or opposed to the respondents' substantive value preference (Interaction 9, Table 2); and (3) the four-way interaction between law/non-law; weak/strong; clear/ambiguous; and opposed/accord decision-making factors (Interaction 12, Table 2).

We will present below only those separate analyses of the noted three- and four-way interactions which helped to specify the precise nature of that interaction. The observable two-way interaction between the orientation and objectivity needs no further analysis (Interaction 4, Table 2). A glance at the germane 2×2 table discloses, as hypothesized, that the law students tended noticeably more toward objectivity.

Next, considering only those people with weak predispositions, the results were as indicated (Tables 3 and 4).

This data would seem to furnish some support for the main hypothesis. In Table 4 we can see that partition of the X^2 data as set out in Table 3 discloses that when the value predisposition is weakly held, there is a significant interaction (at the .05 level of significance) between the orientation (law student/nonlaw

TABLE 3

Effect of Law/Nonlaw Student and Clear/Ambiguous Factors on Objective Decision-Making in the Presence of Weakly Held Values

| | Law Students | | | Nonlaw Students | |
	Clear	Ambiguous		Clear	Ambiguous
OPP	9.7	8.7	OPP	8.7	7.9
	14	10		4	7
ACC	16.6	15	ACC	15	13.5
	13	13		19	15

$X^2 = 5.21$ $p < .30$ d.f. $= 4$

TABLE 4

Partition of Chi-Square in Table 3 (Weak Only)

Interaction	X^2	$p<$	d.f.
1. Total	5.21	.30	4
2. LS/NLS × CL/AMB	0.00	1.00	1
3. LS/NLS × OPP/ACC	4.72	.05	1
4. CL/AMB × OPP/ACC	0.00	1.00	1
5. LS/NLS × CL/AMB × OPP/ACC	0.49	.50	1

student) and the amount of objective decision-making. When the value is strongly held, it might be added, no significant interation can be discerned. This is inconsistent with the first hypothesis.

Continuing with the analysis through partition, it was decided to look at the effective impact of the training factor, since that had been considered a major judicial role-inducing device (Tables 5 and 6).

TABLE 5

Effect of Clear/Ambiguous and Weak/Strong Factors on Objective Decision-Making in the Presence of the Factor of Legal Training

	Weak			Strong	
	Clear	Ambiguous		Clear	Ambiguous
OPP	11.3 / 14	8.8 / 10	OPP	8.4 / 8	6.5 / 3
ACC	16.8 / 13	13.1 / 13	ACC	12.5 / 14	9.7 / 12

$X^2 = 2.93$ $p < .70$ d.f. $= 4$

TABLE 6

Partition of Chi-Square in Table 5 (Law students only)

Interaction	χ^2	p	d.f.
1. Total	2.93	.70	4
2. WK/ST × CL/AMB	0.09	.80	1
3. WK/ST × OPP/ACC	2.27	.20	1
4. CL/AMB × OPP/ACC	0.62	.50	1
5. WK/ST × CL/AMB × OPP/ACC	—0.05		1

Although this partition fails to demonstrate a significant inter-action among the three factors together, the further breakdown shows that there is a noticeable interaction among law students alone between the strength-of-values-held factor and the number of opposed and accord decisions, i.e., objectivity (Interaction 3, Table 6). This finding, then, also runs parallel with the main hypotheses as set forth in Chapter 4. In continuing with hy-pothesis-testing on this factor, an analysis of a similar breakdown among the nonlaw students showed no interaction worth re-porting.

Analysis of the influence of the clarity of precedent factor upon partitioning yields further interesting results (See Tables 7 and 8). Although the chi-square of the total interaction is again not at all significant, a further breakdown again reveals some interactions worthy of note. Analysis shows that when the precedent is clear, then the interaction between the orientation and the objectivity of decision-making is significant at the 10 per cent level (Interaction 3, Table 8). One can also observe some degree of noticeable interaction among the orientation, strength of value, and objectivity of decision factors (Interaction 5, Table 8). These findings, as well as some discussed previously, serve as support for the hypotheses. However, these latter two rea-sonably significant interactions suggest the feasibility of even a further breakdown of the data. In fact, the further breakdown of the clear case data into the separate tables for law students

TABLE 7

Effect of Weak/Strong and Law Student/Nonlaw Student Factors on Objective Decision-Making in the Presence of the Factor of Clarity of Precedent

	Law Student			Nonlaw Student	
	Weak	Strong		Weak	Strong
OPP	10.1	7.7	OPP	8.1	6.1
	14	8		4	6
ACC	17.7	13.5	ACC	14.1	10.7
	13	14		19	10

$\chi^2 = 5.11$ p < .30 d.f. = 4

TABLE 8

Partition of Chi-Square in Table 7 (Clear only)

Interaction	χ^2	p <	d.f.
1. Total	5.11	.30	4
2. LS/NLS × WK/ST	0.01	.95	1
3. LS/NLS × OPP/ACC	2.72	.10	1
4. WK/ST × OPP/ACC	0.00	1.00	1
5. LS/NLS × WK/ST × OPP/ACC	2.38	.20	1

and nonlaw students and for weak and strong predisposition yielded the highest chi-square score in all of the data thus analyzed (See Table 9). The chi-square of 5.04 with one degree of freedom is significant at the 5 per cent level.

This last relationship is strongly and directly supportive of the main hypothesis underlying this study. However, it is important to note explicitly that aside from this last discussed inter-

TABLE 9
Interaction of Law Student/Nonlaw Student and Opposed/Accord Decisions in the Presence of Clear Precedent and Weakly Held Values

	Law Students		Nonlaw Students	
OPP	9.7		8.3	
		14		4
ACC	17.3		14.7	
		13		19

$x^2 = 5.04$ $p < .05$ d.f. $= 1$

action, only one other was statistically significant. This should not be completely discouraging, however. After all, the patterns of observable interaction, though not always at a level of statistical significance, were consistent with most hypotheses and with the theory as discussed in Chapter IV. It doesn't seem unnecessary at this point to reemphasize the fact that this might even be satisfactory in light of our oft-purported aim of simply trying to explore the feasibility of the working theory. However, there is a more sensitive statistical technique which one can use to analyze this same data, i.e., analysis of variance. It will be used to analyze our data in order to recheck the above findings and for other reasons as well.

Analysis of Variance
The main reason for employing analysis of variance does not lie in any deep mistrust of the multidimensional chi-square itself, or in its relationship to the data. Rather, there are several more positive reasons. First, when two tests are available, and the data is occasionally a bit sparse, it would seem to be a helpful verification as to the reported significance of the findings. Secondly,

as has been frequently stated above, this entire work is meant to be exploratory and illustrative in both theory *and method*. As such, then, since two statistical techniques exist which can be used for analysis of the data, it would betray the goals of the study to neglect one of them. Third and finally, the analysis of variance is a more powerful test than the multi-dimensional chi-square.

A first glance at the data, however, seems to indicate a non-applicability of the analysis of variance technique. After all, in observing the cells involved, one would appear to be dealing strictly with frequency information. The units are numbers of people who acted one way or another. There are no scores for individual behavior. Or so it would first appear. Thus, it seems to follow that there is no variation in score to analyze. This is not so. Actually, that which is under study as the dependent variable is the number of objective (OPP) decisions out of the total number of decisions made, under several differing circumstances. In other words, the focus of attention is the *proportion* of objective/nonobjective decisions as the dependent variable. If these are *scored* as 1 and 0 respectively, each cell will yield a mean value equal to the proportion of objective decisions. Thus, each cell will have variation to analyze, and one can then apply the analysis of variance technique.

However, with proportions, variance depends upon the mean. This being the case, and with one prerequisite for the use of analysis of variance being homogeneity of variance, a transformation is needed to make the variance stable and independent of the proportion. The particular transformation employed is the arc-sine transformation. The transformed scores represent means which are equivalent to the respective proportions. Table 10 represents the raw proportions, while Table 11 demonstrates the transformed score.[6] Table 12 is the complete analysis of variance table.

---

[6] C. I. Bliss and D. W. Calhoun, *An Outline of Biometry* (New Haven: Yale Cooperative Corporation, 1954), p. 238.

TABLE 10
Raw Proportion of Objective Decisions: Total Decisions

| | Law Students | | | Nonlaw Students | |
	Clear	Ambig-uous		Clear	Ambig-uous
Strong	.364	.200	Strong	.375	.250
Weak	.519	.435	Weak	.174	.318

TABLE 11
Score After Arc-Sine Transformation

| | Law Students | | | Nonlaw Students | |
	Clear	Ambig-uous		Clear	Ambig-uous
Strong	37.11	26.56	Strong	37.76	30.00
Weak	46.09	41.27	Weak	24.65	34.33

TABLE 12
Significance of Interactions Among Three Main Variables as a Source of Influence Upon Objective Decision-Making: Analysis of Variance

Source of Variation	SS	d.f.	Var. Est.	F.	p. (6.81 sig. at 1%)
(PO/SO) Law/Nonlaw	2556.15	1	2556.15	60.73	.01
(CL/AMB) Clear/Ambiguous	303.12	1	303.12	7.20	.01
(STR/WK) Strong/Weak Values	540.16	1	540.16	12.83	.01
(PO/SO) X (CL/AMB)	738.14	1	738.14	17.54	.01
(PO/SO) X (STR/WK)	2417.13	1	2417.13	57.43	.01
(CL/AMB) X (STR/WK)	1161.17	1	1161.17	27.59	.01
(PO/SO) X (CL/AMB) X (STR/WK)	608.29	1	608.29	14.45	.01
Between Groups Variation	8324.16				
Within Groups Variation	6565.60	156	42.09		
Total	14,889.76	163			

The analysis of variance table indicates that the data is significantly supportive of the hypotheses. It can readily be seen that in this study all variables interact significantly (all beyond the 1 per cent level) in all possible three-way relationships and even in the four-way relationship. *The analysis of variance table indicates that the main source of influence on objective decision-making in an appellate litigation context is the legal training/ nonlegal training (PO/SO) factor (F Ratio of 60.97).* This test also tends to verify the chi-square finding of the importance of the weakness of values factor in triggering the clarity of precedent/role orientation interaction.

Thus, the strong suggestion of a good deal of interaction among the main variables of the theoretical model of the judicial role outlined in Chapter IV is heavily reinforced by the analysis of variance. Upon analysis by two reliable statistical techniques, the data gathered from the 164 students involved in our testing indicates that the hypotheses set forth in the previous chapter have not been disconfirmed. This then is encouraging. It would not be unduly rash to place some confidence in the model as a guide to further research. After all, there is great need to subject the hypotheses to disconfirmation many more times in many different ways before it could be asserted affirmatively with any assurance that they have been confirmed (if it can *ever* really be so stated).

Content Analysis: Detecting Judicial Role

Although the findings indicate the existence of objectivity in the decision-making process, they still cannot be taken to indicate the existence of the judicial role or of precedent orientation. Although the objective decision and the judicial decision are quite similar, they need not be precisely the same. The judicial decision, or that decision which results from the operation of the judicial role, presupposes a certain sophistication with respect to both the guidance and *justification* of the decision by prevailing, pertinent, clear case and statutory law. In a sense it manifests an *explicit deference* of man to law, of whim to continuity.

There would be no way at all to tell from the frequency data used to determine the existence (and the conditions of the existence) of objective decision-making, whether or not an objective decision resulted from a playing of the judicial role by a decision-maker or from the operation of other factors. For instance, given the particular facts and his reaction to them, despite his more abstractly conceived values to the contrary, the decision-maker might simply *reason* his way to a decision opposed to those values. However, reasoning, though part of the appellate process and of judicial role, is not the warp and woof of it. In the judicial process, *the reasoning process must be directly and expressly related to precedent*. And, when the precedent is clear, then the amount of reasoning involved is minimized, and in fact may well be anywhere from negligible to naught.

In developing the decision-making appellate litigation context flavor in this study, care was taken to include a space for the judge to present the reasons for his decision. This was done to serve the purpose in testing that some believe it to serve in the real appellate process, i.e., as an additional relevant institutional constraint upon the judge's free expression of personal values through judicial decision. Moreover, it was included to serve for various types of content analyses. In this study content analysis can assist in discovering whether or not judicial role-playing was responsible for the objective decision-making already observed in the initial sections of this chapter, and whether or not there is any difference between the objective decision-making of the law students and that of the nonlaw students.

In looking back at the data, the reader can see that there were only 22 law students and ten nonlaw students who (we have reason to believe) decided against their values in the Charney case. This number is arrived at by collapsing the strong/weak value factor in the opp/clear cell. In looking at the reasons offered by these judges for their decision, there is a noticeable difference. The law students, as one could expect, are virtually unanimous in their dependence upon and reference to precedent as the foundation for their decision. Some even expressed their rue at having to do so, i.e., go against their own preference for decision because of the law: "It's against my own personal beliefs to do so, but precedent would probably have to be followed here." Only one law student neglected to justify his decision by the existence of the precedent afforded; but even he relied on some law. That is, he utilized some other law that he already knew: "As agent of the hospital, we could probably hold the hospital responsible."

Only half of the nonlaw students, however, even alluded to precedent as the basis of their decision against their own values. They were far more prone to go looking for other reasons—which is a bit strange since they were probably being influenced by the precedent to which they were exposed. One explanation for this might be that the clear precedent actually changed the values of the nonlaw student (i.e., the law was internalized by the layman as his own value), and forced him to seek a rationale to justify this new position. But this is surely not what precedent orientation means. Thus this is a fine illustration of an apparently objective decision being unrelated to the assumption of the judicial role.

Interestingly enough, no two reasoning processes of the nonlaw students who did not assume the judicial role were alike. One of these respondents found in his reading of the case that the hospital was not "directly" responsible and therefore only the nurse ought to be sued. Another, though deciding *mostly* on precedent, also felt that a decision against the hospital was a trifle unfair. That is, there is no reward if the hospital "saves the man's life" but a penalty is levied if they fail. This comes from a respondent, it must be noted, who felt strongly and explicitly in the SVP questionnaire that a hospital was "at fault for hiring the employee" should be suable. A third reasoned that such decisions against hospitals would create a great burden on them in their hiring practices. A fourth argued that the patient assumed the risk; while a fifth reasoned that the glare of adverse publicity was too great a price to pay.

Table 13 demonstrates the frequencies involved in the interaction between the law training factor and the reliance upon legal precedent as a justification for decision. In using Latscha's extension of Finney's Table in testing for significance, we find a significance of difference well beyond the 4 per cent level.[7]

TABLE 13

Judicial Role Playing of Law Students and Nonlaw Students

	Nonlaw	Law
Expressly use precedent to justify objective decision	5	19
Use reasons other than precedent to justify objective decision	4	1

$$N = 29 \quad (p < .04)^8$$

The research technique and this data seem to yield further evidence to support the longstanding theoretical notions of classic American jurisprudential thinking on this subject. However, I want to clarify what the results of this brief content analysis seem to reveal. It could be said that this data demonstrates that the law-trained person assumes the judicial role to a significantly greater degree than he who has not been legally trained. From the chi-square analysis and the analysis of variance, we know that the law students tended to decide more objectively than nonlaw students under the circumstances of the model. This fact, in addition to the fact that almost all of the legally trained students explicitly relied on precedent when they were being objective, while only one-half of the nonlegally trained did so, justifies the statement that judicial role does seem to exist and that it is substantially a function of law-school training. As we have seen, judicial role is manifest as an objective decision justified by

---

[7] R. Latscha, "Tests of Significance in a 2 × 2 Contingency Table: Extension of Finney's Table," *Biometrika*, 40 (June, 1953). This table is ordinarily used when the marginals are less than 20. A 2 × 2 chi-square analysis yielded a score of 3.50 which was almost significant at the .05 level. I did not want to use the chi-square, however, since two of the four expected frequencies were less than 5.

[8] The N is 29 instead of 32 since I could not decipher the handwriting of three of the respondents well enough to include them.

precedent, made in an appellate litigation context, in interaction between precedent orientation and the existence of relevant (to the litigation), clear precedent:

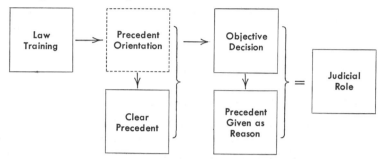

Now, it would be brash to say that this demonstration of the existence of that which we have termed judicial role proves that this is something which operates at all times and under all circumstances in the way which the present study has shown. I simply want to note that this work is indicative that something may well exist which should be recognized by the political scientist in his study of politics as the decision-making process which authoritatively allocates values for the society.

So much for the presentation and analysis of the data. I believe that it is incumbent upon anyone who has espoused the purposes discussed above to present a critique of his own design, data, techniques, and analysis.

A CRITIQUE

For an author to spend a good deal of time criticizing his own work may appear to be a revealing defensiveness. ". . . the lady doth protest too much" is a time-honored caveat to the self-doubter. To avoid elaborating on the deficiencies in one's own efforts is advice well followed in most instances, but it does not have sound application here. Moreover, the intent of self criticism reveals neither any masochistic tendency on the part of the author nor any attempt to precushion external criticism.

Rather, as stated at the outset and throughout this work, the main purposes of the review of the literature (Chapters I and II) and the conduct of the study itself are related to the principal goal: the formulation of a *working* theory which might have organizational and explanatory power, and which will serve a heuristic function for those engaged in research. Thus, where analysis demonstrates that this study falls into one of the categories of weakness discussed immediately below, I shall suggest remedies wherever possible.

How Valid and Reliable is this Study?

The findings show some significant differences and similarities in behavior among the respondents involved in this study—and even between those of each group. However, as in any social scientific venture, the questions are justifiably asked: How accurate a reflection of the whole population are the groups used, and thus how representative are the findings? How does one know that the differences observed were attributable only to the experimentally manipulated factor? How accurate an observation was made? The first two questions involve what is commonly called validity, while the latter involves that which is most commonly termed reliability.

According to one of the most widely used research methods texts in the social sciences,

> The validity of a measuring instrument may be defined as the extent to which differences in scores on it reflect true differences among individuals, groups, or situations in the characteristic which it seeks to measure or true differences in the same individual, groups, or situations from one occasion to another, rather than constant or random errors.[9]

David Krech and Richard S. Crutchfield explain the notion of validity with great clarity and simplicity and point out its interrelationship with reliability:

> The ultimate consideration concerning any measurement technique is its validity, i.e., the extent to which it measures what

---

[9] Selltiz, *op. cit.*, p. 155.

it purports to measure. Invalid measures of beliefs and attitudes are, of course, worthless for the understanding and prediction of behavior. The validity of a technique is dependent in an intimate way upon its reliability, i.e., the extent to which it yields consistent measures.[10]

In a more recent book, Krech and Crutchfield illustrate the distinction as follows: In a quiz given in a psychology class, a student gets 75 per cent correct. The quiz might have been designed (in accord with the intent of the professor) to measure the degree to which the student grasped the fundamental principles of psychology. Each time a similar quiz is given, the same student may get 75 per cent after studying with the same intensity and for the same amount of time. Thus the quiz is a *reliable* indicator, to be sure, *but of what?* Is it an indicator of the student's grasp of psychological principles or his ability to memorize what he reads?[11]

Campbell and Stanley, in noting that almost all writers on this topic comment upon the closeness and interaction between validity and reliability, employ a different conceptualization of their distinction.

Instead of validity and reliability (since validity is the key idea), they prefer to refer to external validity and internal validity respectively. The reason for this is implicit in their conceptualization:

Internal validity is the basic minimum without which any experiment is uninterpretable: did in fact the experimental treatments make a difference in this specific experimental instance? *External validity* asks the question of generalizability: to what populations, settings, treatment variables and measurement variables can this effect be generalized? . . . while *internal validity* is the *sine qua non* and while the question of *external validity*, like the question of inductive inference, is

---

[10] David Krech and Richard S. Crutchfield, *Theory and Problems of Social Psychology* (New York: McGraw-Hill Book Company, 1948), p. 258.

[11] David Krech and Richard S. Crutchfield, *Elements of Psychology* (New York: Alfred A. Knopf, 1958), p. 526.

never completely answerable, the selection of designs strong in both types of validity is obviously our ideal.[12]

Campbell and Stanley list eight different classes of extraneous variables relevant to internal validity which "if not controlled in the experimental or quasi-experimental design, might produce effects confounded with the effect of the experimental stimulus:"

(1) *History*, the specific events occurring between the first and second measurement in addition to the experimental variable.

(2) *Maturation*, processes within the respondents operating as a function of the passage of time *per se* (not specific to the particular events), including growing older, growing hungrier . . .

(3) *Testing*, the effects of taking a test upon the scores of a second testing.

(4) *Instrumentation*, in which changes in the calibration of a measuring instrument or changes in the observers or scorers used may produce changes in the obtained measurements.

(5) *Statistical regression*, operating where groups have been selected on the basis of their extreme scores.

(6) Biases resulting in differential *selection* of respondents for the comparison groups.

(7) *Experimental mortality*, or differential loss of respondents from the comparison groups.

(8) *Selection-maturation interaction*, etc., which in certain of the multiple-group quasi-experimental designs . . . might be mistaken for the effect of the experimental variable.

Relevant to *external validity*, Campbell and Stanley discuss four factors:

(9) The *reactive or interaction effect of testing*, in which a pretest might increase or decrease the respondent's sensitivity or responsiveness to the experimental variable and thus make the results obtained for a pretested population unrepresentative of the effect of the experimental variable for the unpretested universe from which the experimental respondents were selected.

---

[12] Campbell and Stanley, *op. cit.*, p. 175.

(10) *Interaction effects of selection biases* and the experimental variable.

(11) *Reactive effects of experimental arrangements* which would preclude generalization about the effect of the experimental variable upon persons being exposed to it in a non-experimental setting.

(12) *Multiple-treatment inferences,* likely to occur whenever multiple treatments are applied to the respondents, because the effects of prior treatments are not usually erasable.[13]

I propose to subject this study to an even more rigorous analysis than was conducted on any of the individual studies discussed in Chapter I. Campbell and Stanley's criteria can serve as a general guideline. Some of the problems they mention are not applicable to this study design and thus need not be treated.

Also it was felt that some of the criteria could be handled better when combined with others. It is my hope that I can accurately pinpoint some of the more glaring weaknesses in both internal and external validity in this study.

Maturation

This factor has not been controlled in the study, and as a rival plausible hypothesis left undisconfirmed it does injure the internal validity of the findings. Essentially, there are two measurements in time: (1) respondents doing undergraduate work, and (2) respondents after the completion of undergraduate work and doing (in the main) third year law-school work. Note that there is difference in decision-making behavior between the people in these two groups—the experimental group seemed to be significantly more impartial and objective. One cannot be at all certain that this is due to the experimental treatment, i.e., law-school training. After all, in addition to legal training, the experimental group has also experienced several years of simple maturation in age as well as further exposure to reading and academic environment. These factors may be totally or partially responsible for the observed differences.

---

[13] Campbell and Stanley, *op. cit.,* pp. 175–76.

No data was collected to test whether an increase in post-graduate education in any field (graduate work, medical school) might not produce as significant an increase in objectivity as does law-school training. If this proves to be true, one could hardly attribute such an increase to the development of the legal mind without doing some drastic redefining of that concept. Perhaps we might find ourselves with that old shibboleth, the objective, educated mind (*noblesse oblige?*). This, then, might be a fruitful area for future inquiry. At least in any future work on law or the impact of legal training, other post-graduates should comprise a group of respondents so that their decision-making processes might be compared with those of the law students as well as of the general laity.

Testing and Interaction of Testing and X

It is almost axiomatic in the social sciences that one should avoid testing respondents immediately before administering the test which is the crux of the experiment. In such circumstances, the crucial behavior to be measured may be strongly influenced by the first test. This *reactive* effect is obviously undesirable unless reactive effects to prior testing happens to be what the experimenter is interested in observing and measuring. According to Campbell and Stanley:

> The reactive effect can be expected whenever the testing process is in itself a stimulus to change rather than a passive record of behavior. . . . In general, the more novel and motivating the test device, the more reactive one can expect it to be.[14]

Now there can be little doubt but that the initial set of questions in this quasi-experiment (the attitude-evoking questionnaire) may have exerted substantial influence upon the thought process demanded by the subsequent cases to be decided. Any influence exerted would probably have led towards more objective decisions on the part of all the respondents—although the law

---

[14] Campbell and Stanley, *op. cit.*, p. 190.

students may have been more sensitive to what the exercise was all ábout, i.e., what hypotheses were being tested. There is no way of knowing whether any respondent who decided objectively would have done so if he had not known (as he did) that his attitudes in the relevant substantive areas had, just prior to the decision, been made a matter of public record. This is one of the major sources of potential invalidity in the immediate study. Moreover, there does not seem to be any simple nostrum.

One main factor must be eliminated in order to gain both internal and external validity in relationship to the main hypothesis. If the research plan includes the type of questionnaires employed above (designed to tap the *precise* attitudes involved in the cases to be decided), there should be a time lapse between the device which locates the direction and intensity of decisional propensity and the presentation of the cases. This could raise the problem of matching the attitudes of any given respondent with his decision made at a later time, possibly (hopefully) in another place or testing situation. But this can be worked out through various types of deception.

The technique employed in the immediate study (though the most direct method) is crude. A more sophisticated approach might be to utilize already developed and time-tested attitude questionnaires on various topics and then to devise cases which were related to that attitude universe. My method, which reversed this procedure, created many coding difficulties. It will be recalled that in the pretesting it was found that the more general the nature of the questions—and the more broad the attitude universe being demarcated—the less accurate the prediction of how the respondents would want to see the law directed in the fact situation. However this was not nearly so true with the abortion questionnaire (Appendix B-1). There the prediction results were even highly encouraging when an open-ended question about abortion was used. This was probably because the attitude involved was reasonably well pondered or socialized into the minds of the respondents. Established attitude questionnaires often deal with such subject matters. Any that would work would add a certain refinement to this type of study and might allow less interaction between the initial questionnaires and the cases.

Selection and Interaction of Selection on the Experimental Treatment

Campbell and Stanley point out:

> . . . there remains the possibility that the effects validly demonstrated hold only on that unique population from which the experimental and control groups were jointly selected.[15]

In other words, how representative a sample of laymen were the lay respondents? Are Wayne State undergraduates an accurate reflection of the lay population of the United States? The answer is clearly No. Moreover, no attempt was made to develop a representative sample of advanced (third-year) law students. The cooperating schools were chosen on the basis of geographic convenience and access through personal contacts. They include two publicly-supported law schools and two private ones. Two of these are reputed to be among the best in the nation, while two fall nearer to what might be considered the average. Yet, included in this study are no students from the Catholic law schools, small, private bar-passing oriented law schools (e.g., Brooklyn Law School, John Marshall of Chicago, Detroit College of Law), academically poor law schools, nor any of the big three (Harvard, Yale, Columbia). This latter omission is significant for those who would be hopeful that this level of empirical data might be a first step in understanding the decision-making of the justices of the Supreme Court of the United States, as the percentage of our justices who attended one of these three schools is large.

In this type of research, which would hopefully be leading towards a general theory of appellate decision-making, there should be an attempt to achieve a representative ratio between the groups and the population-to-be-generalized-about (appellate judges). With adequate time and pecuniary resources the difficulty is easy enough to resolve.

---

[15] Campbell and Stanley, *op. cit.*, p. 189.

Reactive Arrangements

Perhaps the major charge which could be brought against the particular quasi-experiment developed and described in this book is that the prevailing artificiality of its conditions precludes any valid inferences about legal education, much less than about judicial decision-making. Those who would hold and express this viewpoint might agree with the contention that each item of invalidity expressed above is remediable, but they would probably add that this would be just so much more wasted effort. As far as judicial decision-making is concerned, they would say, it is just not a pencil and paper, hypothetical, obviously social scientifically oriented process. They would argue that while they have not been at all impressed by the results of the Chicago Jury Study Project (because of much the same reasoning) at least the Chicago people used a real jury as well as courtroom and jury-room accoutrements as background for the observed decision-making. These charges cannot be casually sidestepped. They have definite merit and must be handled in order to demonstrate the value in this method, despite the truths in the indictment.

First of all, it is obvious that the best anyone can do in developing controls in a realistic situation is to devise *a simulated appellate decision-making procedure* into which each judge (subject) might be placed on a panel of three or nine. The law and facts, as presented in the briefs and oral argument, would be controlled in much the same way as in the immediate study. The attitudes of the judges would be discovered. Some procedures for this have already been discussed above. Four to six cases could be presented within a half-hour by lawyers or law students, and the judges could then retire either to decide privately and write an opinion, or to have a conference (observed through a one-way screen). The same two-group approach as used in the present study could be employed along with the proposed necessary steps for gaining representativeness. True, the cases, as well as the courtroom procedure, would be greatly simplified. *Over-simplification is a familiar but easily countered criticism of all simulation studies. This is so because the question is not quantitative, as the *over* would imply. The question is only whether the essential components are actually built into the model.

This same defense of the simulation technique is available as a rejoinder to similar criticisms made of the study developed and conducted in this work. After all, the essential components of the judicial decision-making process are discretely operant throughout the study's procedures. Moreover, the real role of the appellate decision-maker is very much a pen and paper exercise— quite unlike the trial jury situation. Campbell and Stanley sum up the arguments for this and the more formal type of simulation study quite well:

> . . . we should keep in mind that the 'successful' sciences such as physics and chemistry make their studies without any attention to representativeness (but with great concern for repeatability by independent researchers). *An ivory-tower artificial laboratory science is a valuable achievement even if unrepresentative, and artificiality may often be essential to the analytic separation of variables fundamental to the achievements of many sciences.*[16]

The italicized section of this last quoted section returns to that which I have stated and restated as the main objective. It is this, then, which must finally lay to rest the criticisms against this type of test. For this was precisely what was attempted.

There is some merit in the charge set out above that the study of law students, no matter how valid and reliable, is not a study of the judicial process. It is true that the appellate adjudicatory process is not handled by law students, but by seasoned attorneys, usually well-versed in private practice, public service, or the teaching of law. This experience, it would be argued, is essential to understanding the judge—and thus the judicial decision. A model which fails to include and test the interaction of this factor is invalid since it is again unrepresentative of that phenomenon which it is being used to reflect and understand. To further bolster their contention, the advocates of this position would do well to advance Paul Freund's maxim

---

[16] Campbell and Stanley, *op. cit.*, p. 188 (emphasis added).

that "The *lawyer* is not the *father* of the judge."[17] This could be used to make the point that if *this* is so, then how can one state that the *law student* is the *father* of the judge?

The reply to this argument is double-pronged. First it must be noted that all judges, in addition to having various professional experiences, have had some type of law training. Almost without exception, the law training is the formal, law-school, Langdell case-method study. This, then, is the first level of data to be thoroughly examined. If a series of studies consistently reveal that law-school seniors are more objective in any type of experiment (whether questionnaire or simulation) than are laymen, then this would surely be damning evidence against those who maintain that there is no truth in the proposition that the judicial process or legal thinking involves impartiality. Similar types of experiments or quasi-experiments can be conducted which would vary other judicial institutional factors (oral arguments, briefs, robes, conferences, written opinions) to see whether the existence of any one or combination of these factors has any effect upon the nature of their decisions among people with and without legal training.

One last major point needs to be mentioned. Professor Robert Harris of the University of Michigan Law School tells of a phenomenon he observed when he was legal clerk to Judge Charles E. Clarke of the U.S. Second Circuit Court of Appeals. His observation concerned that judge's judicial decision-making behavior, particularly in his relationship to the notion of role. According to Harris, Judge Clarke's notion of the importance of precedent would alter from area of law to area of law. In other words, his rating on an eventually developed scale of precedent orientation would not be one which could be applied consistently irrespective of the subject matter of the litigation. In the interview discussed in Chapter II, Justice Tom Clark said that he believed that he should adhere to precedent "strictly" in statutory interpretation cases, but that this wasn't true in constitutional cases.

---

[17] Paul Freund, *On Understanding the Supreme Court* (Boston: Little, Brown and Company, 1949).

He confided though that, even in those latter cases, precedent near the point in litigation could "cause me some trouble." For the limited purposes of this study, neither the notion of degree of such orientations nor the added complication to which Professor Harris has alerted us was included. It is almost needless to say that various methods for isolating and describing variations on this role concept should be devised.

Professor Harris's and Justice Clark's point more clearly demonstrates that there are gradations involved in another of the main variables for which future research must account. This will probably be one of the greatest headaches for future researchers into this field. The problem of gradation of intensity is easily enough solved. Nor should the problem of various shades of clarity cause too much trouble, given the co-operation of law professors for panel work. However, the difficulty involved in developing types and gradations in precedent/situation role postures is inherently great. But this is where we must go.

CONCLUSION

In conclusion then, I hope that the primary and secondary objectives have been achieved in and by the body of this book.

As stated throughout this study, the primary aim has been to wed the new political science judicial behavioral orientation to the theoretical structure propounded in the traditional wisdom of that part of American jurisprudence known as legal realism. It seems to me that only such a merger can effectuate the collection of the type of data which is essential to an understanding of the precise nature and dynamics of the judicial process—whatever this may or may not be.

Before this desirable union can be consummated, though, certain errors in the specific approaches of most of the behavioralists need to be well aired. Moreover, the main factors composing the theory of the modern jurisprudents need to be isolated. In other words, several extant problems in methodology must be scrutinized openly and a workable, empirically-oriented theory devised. I personally believe that much of the existent misdirection of the behavioral research in this field can be corrected only through such steps. If I am right in this belief, I hope that I have assisted in developing some initial steps in these directions. Furthermore, I hope that the work done here can stimulate much further thought along these lines and may be of help in indicating several routes which might prove fruitful upon further refinement.

Secondarily, it was my hope, after explicating and putting into practice the key concepts in my own theoretical scheme, to furnish findings which would serve to confirm a major hypothesis and several subhypotheses about the possible nature of the appellate judicial process. It appears that the theory of the jurisprudents is bolstered by the findings. On the other hand, the views of the main drift of political science judicial behavioralism appear to receive a jolt by them. I must stress that this must not be taken to imply that the findings herein have proved one theory and simultaneously disproved the other. It is simply to say that they tend to support one and not the other.

These findings might indicate one reason why it may be quite possible for researchers to amass data showing a direct relationship between the attitudes or values of an appellate judicial decision-maker and his decisions. Perhaps the various case situations which Schubert and others have used for their description and analysis would be classified by a panel of experts as being ambiguous in precedent. Since this is possible, these cases (or this type of case) might not account for much of a segment of the output of any phase of the American judicial process in general or even the United States Supreme Court process in particular. Moreover, the cases selected for study by political scientists frequently involve factors which might augment or replace the germane substantive value as an effective force in the face of ambiguous precedent, e.g., strong external political or social pressures. This too remains to be seen.

These findings might also help to explain, at least partially, why some 90 per cent of all cases appealed to the Supreme Court are denied review. After all, if the precedent is clear and the appeal is taken, why should the Court, given their precedent orientation, grant review? We have seen that the layman can detect clear precedent and constrain his own predilection to act in a given way even when the precedent would have him act contrary to his value leaning. Furthermore, great clarity of precedent might well account for a tremendous amount of potential appellate litigation which never gets to the appeal stage. In other words, much conflict might be resolved by clear precedent and never carried further despite the personal desires of the attorneys and of the majority of judges on the court. Clearly, the limiting of analysis of the process to only those few cases which manage to get appealed, and of those to the few which are accepted for review, might well be stacking the data so as to eliminate the operation of two of the major elements in the process, i.e., precedent orientation and clarity of precedent. The findings support the many people who have been making this argument against many political scientists and political pamphleteers for years.

Of course the data upon which these questions are based have a peculiarity. This peculiarity might eventually prove to be an effective one and thus seriously limit the data from being relevant to the type of case usually analyzed by the judicial behavioralist. A close look at the two cases used for analysis will disclose the fact that they are what might be termed statutory interpretation cases. The usual stock-in-trade case used for analysis by the judicial behavioralist, however, is the judicial review case. Now, it appears to me, political science has almost completely ignored this distinction in its study of the interaction between the judicial process, the judicial decision, and politics. To political science, the main political role of the appellate courts comes in judicial review. As one prominent political scientist would have it:

> . . . the most important function of the Supreme Court is the settlement of fundamentally political issues through the medium of judicial review. . . .[18]

However, I am not too sure that this is so. After all, in most of the cases, the Court has put the stamp of *approval* on the legislative action under question. According to Henry Abraham:

[18] John R. Schmidhauser, *The Supreme Court: Its Personalities, Politics, and Procedure* (New York: Holt, Rinehart and Winston, 1960), p. 57.

(The United States Supreme Court) has to date [1961–62] declared but 89 provisions of *federal* laws unconstitutional out of a total of over 65,000 public and private laws passed.[19]

Thus, the Court has actually redistributed values authoritatively (i.e., returned the distribution to the *status quo ante*) in only a very few cases. True, a legitimizing act is a political one (although quite indirectly), but actually we don't even know that the legitimacy function exists at all. On the other hand, statutory interpretation is the word of the Court as to precisely what goes to precisely whom, when, and how. Yet political science has ignored this area almost entirely. It surely has not made much specific mention or study of it. Is the distinction in what the Court is doing significant in affecting its objectivity? In other words, is the Court more objective in statutory interpretation than in judicial review? Perhaps it is less objective? In any event, this too must be studied. Again, the preliminary findings herein would seem to justify such a research undertaking.

What I have propounded is a working theory whose factors are simply those which have been theorized for some time as being the major operable ones in the appellate judicial process. Modern research and analytic techniques cannot ignore them and then deny their theoretical efficacy. Inferences made and conclusions drawn without a thorough study of possible existence and interaction of these factors can only be classified as wild and unworthy of serious consideration. Much more imagination needs to be stirred and much hard digging needs be done before we can begin to present verified propositions about the nature of the appellate judicial process and its impact on the formulation of public policy.

Finally, aside from these stated academic reasons, there is another major reason why this area of study ought to be researched as systematically and rigorously as possible. The reason is one of function to the society in which we all live. After all, we who study the judicial process and the law must keep in mind that we are studying and writing about the cardinal means

---

[19] Henry J. Abraham, *The Judicial Process* (New York: Oxford University Press, 1962), p. 252.

of social control within our society and possibly in any society. The so-called myth of judicial objectivity may only be a myth in the symbols used to describe a real and important social phenomenon. To disprove that the sun is not pulled across the sky by Apollo does not mean that there is no sun . . . nor does it disprove the fact that man sees the sun as moving across the sky. That we have disproved Lord Coke's view that judges *find* the law does not mean that the judicial process does not differ from other governmental processes or that this difference is not a functional one for societal stability. This is not to say that if we find that no difference exists, we should then bury our facts (though maybe we should) for fear that this knowledge might disturb a precious equilibrium. However, it is to say that our inquiry has more than academic interest and ought to be conducted with utmost scientific detachment, zeal, and rigor—and that we must not be prone to the spreading of pseudoscientific rumors about the nature of the judicial process.

These are my pleas. These are the several reasons for my pleas. Ours is a solemn but exciting task . . . not to be taken lightly or without hope of shedding helpful light.

Appendices

APPENDIX A

A-1

Clarke v. Slade

Rodney Slade owned a series of multi-purpose camping sites for various forms of transportation. He solicited the business of trailers, microbuses, trucks, and cars. He would rent cots to truck drivers to set up in the back of their trucks, tents with cots in them for automobile drivers, space for microbus drivers and trailer owners to occupy, etc. Aside from the space and cots, other services supplied included a coffee shop and protection of the sleepers. These were spaced at intervals along the Turn-pike, and he charged $4.00 per day and $100 per month for trailer sites. (This was more than double the average rate for such a facility throughout the United States.) The State Rent Control Board has jurisdiction to regulate rents for "apartment houses, tenement buildings, hotels, motels, inns, and similar places of lodging." The statute conferring such power was ruled to be constitutional in 1957 by both the state and U.S. Supreme Courts. This state is very similar to Michigan in its economic circumstances.

Stephen Clarke, a trailer owner and resident of Slade Over-niter #5, brought action against Slade before the Rent Control Board in order to have them declare Slade's rates excessive and to compel him to lower his rents. The Board ordered that the rental be lowered to a maximum of $2.75 per day and $60 per month. Slade appeals the decision of the Board to the Supreme Court of the state.

The brief for Clarke stands upon the case of *State* v. *Reginald's Trailer Camps* wherein the Supreme Court held that the State Rent Control Board's jurisdiction extended to trailer camps as falling within the meaning of "similar places of lodging." Slade's main argument is that his business was that of "protecting travelers" and quite distinct from that of an apartment house owner or motel owner and trailer camp owners.

Decide this case as a good Justice of the state Supreme Court should.

The ruling of the Board is reversed (for Slade) _____

The ruling of the Board is affirmed (for Clarke) _____

Reasons:

A-2

State v. Claire

Dr. Claire committed an abortion upon a long time patient of his, Miss D, because in his opinion: "It was necessary to do so." Miss D had only been out of the State Mental Hospital for about 1 year when she became pregnant. According to the testimony of several psychoanalysts and psychiatrists at the trial, Miss D, in her mental condition, would most probably have been compelled to return to the Hospital for extended treatment upon the birth of her illegitimate child. The experts were in total agreement on this point. Dr. Claire was convicted and appeals to the Supreme Court.

The relevant state statute reads:

> Whosoever administers drugs or applies instruments to a pregnant woman, with or without her consent, for the purpose of bringing about a miscarriage, is guilty of a felony unless such is necessary to preserve the life or health of the woman.

The only pertinent case in the jurisdiction is that of *State* v. *Black* (1960). In that case, the state Supreme Court reversed the conviction of a doctor who had committed an abortion when "necessity" was deemed to have been established in a case where expert medical testimony was unanimous that "the birth process would cause the woman to have a severe nervous breakdown" and that "health certainly means mental as well as physical well-being."

Decide this case as a good judge of the Supreme Court should:

Affirm the conviction of Dr. Claire

(Against Dr. Claire) _____

Reverse the conviction of Dr. Claire

(For Dr. Claire) _____

Reasons:

A-3

Charney v. St. Mary's Mercy Hospital

[Mr. Charney was seriously injured in an automobile accident. He was rushed to the St. Mary's Mercy Hospital where an emergency blood transfusion was found to be necessary. In the handling of the blood, one of the nurses of the hospital made an error and supplied the doctor with the wrong type of blood. It was proved at the trial that this error was directly responsible for the death of Mr. Charney. Charney's widow sued the hospital for negligence for $100,000. Negligence was clearly established by the evidence, and] the jury returned a verdict for the plaintiff, Mrs. Charney. The hospital appeals.

The law of the jurisdiction is based on several cases. *Karrin* v. *Curtis* (1940) held, in reversing a jury verdict for the plantiff, that a charitable organization is not responsible for damages occasioned by the negligence of its employees, if the negligent act is done while the employee was pursuing the course of employment. The case of *Rick* v. *Castberg* (1958) held that an overdose of barbiturates given to the plantiff-patient by an intern in a hospital did not constitute a breach of warranty in a sale and, therefore, the private hospital employing the intern was not liable for damages to the plaintiff.

Decide this case as a good judge of the state Supreme Court should:

Reverse the lower court decision
                      (for the hospital) _____

Affirm the lower court decision
                      (for Charney in
                      the full amount
                      that the jury
                      agreed upon) _____

Reasons:

A-4
Arthur v. St. Mary's Mercy Hospital

[Mr. Arthur was seriously injured in an automobile accident. He was rushed to the St. Mary's Mercy Hospital where an emergency blood transfusion was found to be necessary. In the handling of the blood, one of the nurses of the hospital made an error and supplied the doctor with the wrong type of blood. It was proved at the trial that this error was directly responsible for the death of Mr. Arthur. Arthur's widow sued the hospital for $100,000. The jury returned a verdict for the plaintiff, Mrs. Arthur, in the full amount sought. The hospital appeals.]

There is a state statute which reads as follows:

> No charitable institution shall be held liable for damages in a suit at law brought about by the negligence of its employees, whether such negligent act was done during the course of the employment or not.

However, the case of *Williams* v. *Fleming Hospital* (1956) held that a hospital was liable for breach of warranty where a person suffered severe food poisoning in the hospital cafeteria. The law of the state is that goods sold carry an automatic warranty that the seller must compensate financially for damages caused by the fact that such goods were not fit for the purposes for which they were sold. The case of *City of Richards* v. *Dawson* (1961) held that the sale of blood (all blood used in this hospital must be paid for) could not be considered to be a "sale" within the meaning of the City Sales Tax.

Decide this case as a good judge of the state Supreme Court should:

Reverse the lower court decision
(for the hospital) _____

Affirm the lower court decision
(for Arthur in
the full amount
that the jury
agreed upon) _____

Reasons:

APPENDIX B

B-1

Abortion

1. What are your *personal* views on abortion?

2. Do you believe that abortion is justified in order to protect the life of the mother?

3. Might it be justified in order to safeguard the physical as well as the mental health of the mother? Only the physical? Only the mental health?

4. Would your answer to question 3 remain the same if it were only probable (rather than certain) that the physical or mental health of the mother would be put in jeopardy by the birth process?

5. Do you believe that abortion ought to be legalized to include any situation where the mother-to-be just wants to have it done because she would prefer not having the child?

— ☐ 4

— ☐ 3

— ☐ 2

— ☐ 1

B-2

Responsibilities of Charities

1. What are your *personal* views as to whether charities ought to have certain privileges, under the law, that other corporations do not have?

2. Do you think that charities, unlike most other organizations, ought to be tax exempt?

3. It is the law that corporations are liable in money damages to a person injured through a negligent act of an employee of the corporation when that act was done while the employee was carrying out the work of the corporation. Do you think that this law ought to be applicable to charitable corporations (charities)?

4. Do you consider:
   the Salvation Army to be a charity?
   hospitals?
   (a) municipal hospitals?
   (b) religious hospitals?
   (c) private hospitals?
   (d) federal hospitals?
   the Red Cross?

5. What if someone was seriously injured or killed by the negligent act of an employee of a hospital but that this occurred while the injured or killed person was receiving the benefits of the hospital—should the hospital or just the employee be liable for money damages, or neither?

6. If the negligent employee was an intern or a hospital nurse, should the hospital be suable in court for money damages or just the nurse or the intern?
   Would your answer hold true for each type of hospital listed in Question 4?

$$- \square\ 4$$
$$- \square\ 3$$
$$- \square\ 2$$
$$- \square\ 1$$

APPENDIX C

In this part, we are asking that you play the role of a legislator. On the next pages are 7 factual situations. Read each carefully. After you have read each, ask yourself the following questions:

If I were a legislator and could make the law, which party in this case would I want to see the law favor?

Answer this question by checking the appropriate box at the left of the party who you would want to see the law favor. For example, in a case between Smith and Jones, if you would want to see the law in Smith's favor, your response would be:

☑—for Smith

☐—for Jones

APPENDIX D

Panelists Who Rated Substantive Value Predisposition

1. Sheldon Appleton, BA, New York University, 1955; MA, PhD (Political Science), University of Minnesota, 1960. Assistant Professor of Political Science, Oakland University, 1961–to date.

2. Donald C. Hildum, BA, Princeton University, 1954; PhD (Psychology) Harvard University, 1960. Instructor, Case Institute of Technology; Assistant Professor of Psychology, Oakland University, 1961–to date.

3. Nathan Simons, Jr., BA, St. Mary's University, 1950; PhD (Economics), The Ohio State University, 1962. Assistant Professor of Economics, Oakland University, 1961–64; Assistant Director of Research, Bureau of Public Roads, United States Department of Commerce, 1964–to date.

4. Baljit Singh, PhD (Political Science) University of Maryland, 1961. Assistant Professor of Political Science, Wayne State University, 1962–63; Assistant Professor of Political Science, Michigan State University, 1963–to date.

APPENDIX E

Predisposition Rating Sheet

_____

Rater

Sheet No.: _____

Questionnaire Number Value Wt.	Predisposed for:		Questionnaire Number Value Wt.	Predisposed for:
#			#	
4 3 2 1 ___ doctor	___ state		4 3 2 1 ___ doctor	___ state
4 3 2 1 ___ hospital	___ patient		4 3 2 1 ___ hospital	___ patient
4 3 2 1 ___ lifeguard	___ wife		4 3 2 1 ___ lifeguard	___ wife
___ 4 3 2 1 ___ landlord	___ tenant		___ 4 3 2 1 ___ landlord	___ tenant
4 3 2 1 ___ doctor	___ state		4 3 2 1 ___ doctor	___ state
4 3 2 1 ___ hospital	___ patient		4 3 2 1 ___ hospital	___ patient
4 3 2 1 ___ lifeguard	___ wife		4 3 2 1 ___ lifeguard	___ wife
___ 4 3 2 1 ___ landlord	___ tenant		___ 4 3 2 1 ___ landlord	___ tenant
4 3 2 1 ___ doctor	___ state		4 3 2 1 ___ doctor	___ state
4 3 2 1 ___ hospital	___ patient		4 3 2 1 ___ hospital	___ patient
4 3 2 1 ___ lifeguard	___ wife		4 3 2 1 ___ lifeguard	___ wife
___ 4 3 2 1 ___ landlord	___ tenant		___ 4 3 2 1 ___ landlord	___ tenant
4 3 2 1 ___ doctor	___ state		4 3 2 1 ___ doctor	___ state
4 3 2 1 ___ hospital	___ patient		4 3 2 1 ___ hospital	___ patient
4 3 2 1 ___ lifeguard	___ wife		4 3 2 1 ___ lifeguard	___ wife
___ 4 3 2 1 ___ landlord	___ tenant		___ 4 3 2 1 ___ landlord	___ tenant
4 3 2 1 ___ doctor	___ state		4 3 2 1 ___ doctor	___ state
4 3 2 1 ___ hospital	___ patient		4 3 2 1 ___ hospital	___ patient
4 3 2 1 ___ lifeguard	___ wife		4 3 2 1 ___ lifeguard	___ wife
___ 4 3 2 1 ___ landlord	___ tenant		___ 4 3 2 1 ___ landlord	___ tenant
4 3 2 1 ___ doctor	___ state		4 3 2 1 ___ doctor	___ state
4 3 2 1 ___ hospital	___ patient		4 3 2 1 ___ hospital	___ patient
4 3 2 1 ___ lifeguard	___ wife		4 3 2 1 ___ lifeguard	___ wife
___ 4 3 2 1 ___ landlord	___ tenant		___ 4 3 2 1 ___ landlord	___ tenant
4 3 2 1 ___ doctor	___ state		4 3 2 1 ___ doctor	___ state
4 3 2 1 ___ hospital	___ patient		4 3 2 1 ___ hospital	___ patient
4 3 2 1 ___ lifeguard	___ wife		4 3 2 1 ___ lifeguard	___ wife
___ 4 3 2 1 ___ landlord	___ tenant		___ 4 3 2 1 ___ landlord	___ tenant
4 3 2 1 ___ doctor	___ state		4 3 2 1 ___ doctor	___ state
4 3 2 1 ___ hospital	___ patient		4 3 2 1 ___ hospital	___ patient
4 3 2 1 ___ lifeguard	___ wife		4 3 2 1 ___ lifeguard	___ wife
___ 4 3 2 1 ___ landlord	___ tenant		___ 4 3 2 1 ___ landlord	___ tenant
4 3 2 1 ___ doctor	___ state		4 3 2 1 ___ doctor	___ state
4 3 2 1 ___ hospital	___ patient		4 3 2 1 ___ hospital	___ patient
4 3 2 1 ___ lifeguard	___ wife		4 3 2 1 ___ lifeguard	___ wife
___ 4 3 2 1 ___ landlord	___ tenant		___ 4 3 2 1 ___ landlord	___ tenant

APPENDIX F

Panelists Who Rated Clarity of Precedent

1. Lionel Frankel, Associate Professor of Law, Wayne State University Law School. BA, Ursinus College, 1953; LLB, Yale University, 1956; LLM, New York University, 1962. Admitted to the Bar of New York, 1956. Instructor, The Ohio State University, 1956.

2. Robert Harris, Associate Professor of Law, University of Michigan, School of Law. BA, Wesleyan University, 1953; LLB, Yale University, 1956. Admitted to the Bar of Connecticut, 1956. Clerk to Judge Charles Clark, Second Circuit Court of Appeals of the United States; Assistant Professor, George Washington University, 1958–59.

3. Jerold Israel, Assistant Professor of Law, University of Michigan, School of Law. BBA, Western Reserve University, 1956; LLB, Yale University, 1959. Admitted to the Bar of Ohio, 1959. Law Clerk to Mr. Justice Stewart, United States Supreme Court, 1959–61.

4. Richard S. Miller, Professor of Law, Wayne State University Law School. BS, LLB, Boston University, 1951, 1956; LLM, Yale University, Sterling-Ford Fellow, 1959. Admitted to the Bars of Massachusetts, 1956; Michigan, 1961. Teaching Fellow, Boston University, 1956–57. Instructor, Boston College, 1957–58.

APPENDIX G
Experts' Rating Sheet: Clarity of Precedent

Name of Rater

Note: Please circle your choice

CASE A	0	1	2	3
CASE B	0	1	2	3
CASE C	0	1	2	3
CASE D	0	1	2	3
CASE E	0	1	2	3
CASE F	0	1	2	3
CASE G	0	1	2	3
CASE H	0	1	2	3
CASE I	0	1	2	3
CASE J	0	1	2	3

Key:

0 = Highly Ambiguous (Precedent is no guide to deciding for either party)

1 = Ambiguous (Though ambiguous, the precedent does seem to tend for decision in favor of:).

2 = Quite Clear (The precedent, though a bit off point, quite clearly leads one to decide in favor of:).

3 = Perfectly Clear (The precedent leaves no doubt as to whom the court must decide. Judgment for:).

Comment: (What changes in either the statement of fact or law in any or all of the cases you have rated would you suggest in order to make the precedent *perfectly clear* in favor of one of the parties? What changes would you suggest to make it *highly ambiguous*?)

APPENDIX H

Northwestern University, Department of Political Science

The following questionnaire is part of a study being conducted by the Department of Political Science in cooperation with the Department of Sociology and the School of Law. It consists of four different sections. We would greatly appreciate your assistance in working through it. All in all it should not take much more than 35 minutes of your time. Your name is not required.

Please progress through the questionnaire in a page-by-page fashion. Do not look ahead at subsequent pages and do not turn back once you have completed a page.

We believe that you will find the substantive sections of the questionnaire to be an interesting and absorbing exercise. Thank you again for your help on this project.

APPENDIX I

The following four pages present four different cases for you to decide. You are to place yourself in the *role* of a *Justice* of the Supreme Court of the state deciding the case. Please read each case very carefully and decide it as you *believe a good judge should decide* it. Indicate your decision by placing a check mark in the blank space to the right of the alternative of your choice. Thus, if you want to decide in favor of Smith, you would indicate your decision so:

Judgment for Smith___V_____

Judgment for Jones_____

After you have indicated your choice, please discuss the reasons for your decision in the space allotted for this below the case.

Bibliography

Books

Bales, Robert. *Interaction Process Analysis: A Method for the Study of Small Groups.* Cambridge: Harvard University Press, 1950.

Beutel, Frederick K. *Some Potentialities of Experimental Jurisprudence as a New Branch of Social Science.* Lincoln: University of Nebraska Press, 1957.

Black, Charles. *The People and the Court.* New York: The Macmillan Company, 1960.

Bliss, C. I., and Calhoun, D. W. *An Outline of Biometry.* New Haven: Yale Cooperative Corporation, 1954.

Campbell, Angus, et al. *The American Voter.* New York: John Wiley and Sons, 1960.

Cardozo, Benjamin N. *Growth of the Law.* New Haven: Yale University Press, 1924.

————. *Paradoxes of Legal Science.* New York: Columbia University Press, 1928.

Cartwright, Dorwin, and Zander, Alvin (eds.). *Group Dynamics: Research and Theory.* Evanston, Illinois: Row, Peterson Company, 1960.

Chapin, Francis S. *Experimental Designs in Sociological Research.* New York: Harper and Brothers, 1947.

Charlesworth, James C. (ed.). *The Limits of Behavioralism in Political Science.* Philadelphia: The American Academy of Political and Social Science, 1962.

161

Edwards, Allen L. *Statistical Analysis*. New York: Rinehart and Company, 1946.

————. *Statistical Methods for the Behavioral Sciences*. New York: Rinehart and Company, 1954.

Festinger, Leon, and Katz, Daniel (eds.). *Research Methods in the Behavioral Sciences*. New York: Dryden Press, 1953.

Frank, Jerome. *Law and the Modern Mind*. New York: Coward-McCann, 1930.

————. *Courts on Trial*. Princeton: Princeton University Press, 1950.

Frank, John P. *Marble Palace*. New York: Alfred A. Knopf, 1958.

Freund, Paul. *On Understanding the Supreme Court*. Boston: Little, Brown and Company, 1949.

Gage, N. L. (ed.). *Handbook of Research on Teaching*. Chicago: Rand McNally & Company, 1963.

Gluckman, Max. *The Judicial Process of the Barotse of Northern Rhodesia*. Manchester: Manchester University Press, 1954.

Gosnell, Harold. *Getting Out the Vote*. Chicago: University of Chicago Press, 1927.

Gray, John C. *The Nature and Sources of Law*. New York: Columbia University Press, 1909.

Gross, Neil, et al. *Explorations in Role Analysis*. New York: John Wiley and Sons, 1958.

Guetzkow, Harold. *Simulation in the Social Sciences*. Englewood Cliffs: Prentice-Hall, 1962.

Hall, Jerome. *Living Law of Democratic Society*. Indianapolis: Bobbs-Merrill Company, 1949.

Hand, Learned. *The Bill of Rights*. Cambridge: Harvard University Press, 1960.

Hoebel, E. Adamson. *The Law of Primitive Man*. Cambridge: Harvard University Press, 1955.

Holmes, Oliver W. *The Common Law*. Boston: Little, Brown and Company, 1881.

Hyneman, Charles. *The Study of Politics*. Urbana: University of Illinois Press, 1960.

Kaplan, Abraham. *The Conduct of Inquiry*. San Francisco: Chandler Publishing Company, 1964.

Krech, David, and Crutchfield, Richard S. *Elements of Psychology.* New York: Alfred A. Knopf, 1961.
————. *Theory and Problems of Social Psychology.* New York: McGraw-Hill Book Company, 1948.

Lasswell, Harold D. *The Future of Political Science.* New York: Atherton Press, 1963.

Levi, Edward. *Introduction to Legal Reasoning.* Chicago: University of Chicago Press, 1949.

Llewellyn, Karl. *The Common Law Tradition.* Boston: Little, Brown and Company, 1960.

MacDougal, Myres D., and associates. *Studies in the World Public Order.* New Haven: Yale University Press, 1960.

Margenau, Henry. *The Nature of Physical Reality.* New York: McGraw-Hill Book Company, 1950.

Matthews, Donald R. *The Social Background of Political Decision Makers.* Garden City, New York: Doubleday and Company, 1954.
————. *U.S. Senators and Their World.* Chapel Hill: University of North Carolina Press, 1960.

Pearson, Drew, and Allen, R. S. *The Nine Old Men.* New York: Doubleday, Doran and Company, 1936.

Pekelis, Alexander M. *Law and Social Action.* Ithaca: Cornell University Press, 1950.

Peltason, Jack. *Federal Courts in the Political Process.* New York: Random House, 1955.
————. *Fifty Eight Lonely Men.* New York: Harcourt Brace, 1961.

Pound, Roscoe. *An Introduction to the Philosophy of Law.* New Haven: Yale University Press, 1922.

Pritchett, C. Herman. *The Roosevelt Court: A Study in Judicial Politics and Values, 1937–1947.* New York: The Macmillan Company, 1948.

Radin, Max. *Law as Logic and Experience.* New Haven: Yale University Press, 1940.

Roche, John P. *Courts and Rights.* New York: Random House, 1961.

Rodell, Fred. *Woe Unto You Lawyers!* New York: Reynal and Hitchcock, 1939.

Rose, Arnold M. *Theory and Method in the Social Sciences.* Minneapolis: University of Minnesota Press, 1954.

Rosenblum, Victor G. *Law as a Political Instrument.* New York: Doubleday and Company, 1955.

Schientag, Bernard. *The Personality of the Judge.* New York: The Association of the Bar of the City of New York, Committee on Post-Admission Legal Education, 1944.

Schmidhauser, John R. *The Supreme Court.* New York: Holt, Rinehart and Winston, 1960.

Schubert, Glendon. *Constitutional Politics.* New York: Holt, Rinehart and Winston, 1960.

————. (ed.). *Judicial Decision-Making.* New York: The Free Press of Glencoe, 1963.

————. *Quantitative Analysis of Judicial Behavior.* Glencoe: The Free Press, 1959.

Schwartz, Bernard. *The Professor and the Committee.* New York: Alfred A. Knopf, 1959.

————.*The Supreme Court: Constitutional Revolution in Retrospect.* New York: The Ronald Press, 1957.

Selltiz, Claire, et al. *Research Methods in Social Relations.* rev. ed. New York: Henry Holt and Company, 1959.

Senders, Virginia. *Measurement and Statistics.* New York: Oxford University Press, 1958.

Snedecor, G. W. *Statistical Methods.* 3rd ed. Ames: Iowa Collegiate Press, 1940.

Snyder, Richard, Bruck, H. W., and Sapin, Burton. *Foreign Policy Decision-Making.* New York: The Free Press of Glencoe, 1963.

Taper, Bernard. *Gomillion Versus Lightfoot.* New York: McGraw-Hill Book Company, 1962.

Torgeson, Warren. *Theory and Methods of Scaling.* New York: John Wiley and Sons, 1958.

Truman, David B. *The Governmental Process.* New York: Alfred A. Knopf, 1951.

————. *The Congressional Party.* New York: John Wiley and Sons, 1959.

Ulmer, S. Sidney (ed.). *Introductory Readings in Political Behavior.* Chicago: Rand McNally & Company, 1960.

Underwood, Benton J., et al. *Elementary Statistics.* New York: Appleton-Century-Crofts, Inc., 1954.

Verba, Sidney. *Small Groups and Political Behavior.* Princeton: Princeton University Press, 1961.

Vose, Clement E. *Caucasians Only.* Berkeley and Los Angeles: University of California Press, 1959.

Wahlke, John C., and Eulau, Heinz (eds.). *Legislative Behavior.* Glencoe: The Free Press, 1959.

Wahlke, John C., et al. *The Legislative System.* New York: John Wiley and Sons, 1962.

Wasserstrom, Richard. *The Judicial Decision.* Stanford: Stanford University Press, 1961.

Wechsler, Herbert. *Principles, Politics, and Fundamental Law.* Cambridge: Harvard University Press, 1961.

Westin, Alan F. (ed.). *The Supreme Court: Views from the Inside.* New York: W. W. Norton and Company, 1961.

White, Ralph K., and Lippitt, Ronald. *Autocracy and Democracy.* New York: Harper and Brothers, 1960.

Young, Roland. *Approaches to the Study of Politics.* Evanston: Northwestern University Press, 1958.

Articles

Becker, Theodore L. "Inquiry into a School of Thought in the Judicial Behavior Movement," *Midwest Journal of Political Science,* 7 (August, 1963), 254–66.

Bevan, William, et al. "Jury Behavior as a Function of the Prestige of the Foreman and the Nature of his Leadership," *Journal of Public Law,* 7 (1958), 419.

Broeder, Dale W. "The University of Chicago Jury Project," *Nebraska Law Review,* 38 (1959), 744.

Campbell, Donald T., and Stanley, Julian, "Experimental and Quasi-Experimental Designs for Research on Teaching," in

N. L. Gage (ed.), *Handbook of Research on Teaching*. Chicago: Rand McNally & Company, 1963. Pp. 171–246.

Campbell, Donald T. "From Description to Experimentation: Interpreting Trends as Quasi-Experiments," in C. W. Harris (ed.), *Problems in Measuring Change*. Madison: University of Wisconsin Press, 1963.

Cook, Walter W. "The Logical and Legal Bases of the Conflicts of Law," *Yale Law Journal*, 33 (1929), 467.

————. " 'Substance' and 'Procedure' in the Conflicts of Law," *Yale Law Journal*, 42 (1933), 333.

Cowan, Thomas A. "Decision Theory in Law, Science and Technology," *Rutgers Law Review*, 17 (1963), 499.

Dahl, Robert. "The Role of the Supreme Court as National Policy Maker," *Journal of Public Law*, 6 (1957), 297.

————. "The Behavioral Approach," *American Political Science Review*, 55 (December, 1961), 763–72.

Danelski, David J. "The Influence of the Chief Justice in the Decisional Process," in Walter F. Murphy and C. Herman Pritchett (eds.), *Courts, Judges and Politics*. New York: Random House, 1961. Pp. 497–508.

————. "Values as Variables in Judicial Decision-Making: Notes Toward a Theory." Paper delivered at 1964 Midwest Conference of Political Scientists, Madison, Wisconsin.

Eckert, R. E., and Mills, H. C. "International Attitudes and Related Academic and Social Factors," *Journal of Educational Sociology*, 9 (1935), 142–53.

Fay, P. J., and Middleton, W. C. "Certain Factors Related to Liberal and Conservative Attitudes of College Students: III. Parental Membership in Certain Organization," *Journal of Social Psychology*, 12 (1944), 55–69.

Fisher, Franklin M. "On the Existence and Linearity of Perfect Predictors in 'Content Analysis'," *MULL*, 60M (March, 1960), 1–9.

Frank, Jerome. "Judicial Fact-finding and Psychology," *Ohio State Law Journal*, 14 (1953), 183.

Grossman, Joel B. "Role Playing and the Analysis of Judicial

Behavior: The Case of Mr. Justice Frankfurter," *Journal of Public Law*, 11 (1962), 285.

Hart, Henry M. "Forward: The Time Chart of the Justices," *Harvard Law Review*, 73 (1959), 84.

Hyneman, Charles. "Legislative Experience of Illinois Lawmakers," *University of Chicago Law Review*, 3 (1935), 104.

_____. "Who Makes Our Laws?" *Political Science Quarterly*, 55 (December, 1940), 556–81.

Jackson, Robert. "The Supreme Court as a Political Institution," reproduced in Alan F. Westin (ed.). *The Supreme Court: Views from Inside*. New York: W. W. Norton, 1961.

Kort, Fred. "Predicting Supreme Court Decisions Mathematically: A Quantitative Analysis of the Right to Counsel Cases," *American Political Science Review*, 51 (1957), 1–12.

Latscha, R. "Tests of Significance in a 2 × 2 Contingency Table: Extension of Finney's Table," *Biometrika*, 40 (June, 1953).

Loevinger, Lee. "Jurimetrics—The Next Step Forward," *University of Minnesota Law Review*, 33 (1949), 455.

Mendelson, Wallace. "The Neo-Behavioral Approach to the Judicial Process: A Critique," *American Political Science Review*, 57 (September, 1963), 593–603.

Miller, Arthur S., and Howell, Ronald F. "The Myth of Neutrality in Constitutional Adjudication," *University of Chicago Law Review*, 27 (1960), 661.

Nagel, Stuart. "Off-the-Bench Judicial Attitudes," in Glendon Schubert (ed.), *Judicial Decision-Making*. New York: The Free Press of Glencoe, 1963.

_____. "Political Party Affiliation and Judges' Decisions," *American Political Science Review*, 55 (December, 1961), 843–50.

_____. "Political Parties and Judicial Review in American History," *Journal of Public Law*, 11 (1962), 328.

_____. "Sociometric Relations Among American Courts," *Southwestern Social Science Quarterly*, 43 (September, 1962), 136–42.

_____. "Testing Relations between Judicial Characteristics

and Judicial Decision-Making," *Western Political Quarterly,* 15 (September, 1962), 425–37.

——. "Applying Correlation Analysis to Case Prediction," *Texas Law Review* 42 (October, 1964), 1006–17.

Neiman, L. J., and Hughes, J. W. "The Problems of the Concept of Role—A Re-survey of the Literature," *Social Forces,* 30 (1951), 141–49.

Pollak, Louis H. "Racial Discrimination and Judicial Integrity: A Reply to Professor Wechsler," *University of Pennsylvania Law Review,* 108 (1959), 1.

Remington, F. J., and Rosenblum, V. G. "The Criminal Law and the Legislative Process," *Law Forum,* 481 (1960).

Rubin-Rabson, Grace. "Several Correlates of a Conservatism-Liberalism Attitude Scale," *Journal of Social Psychology,* 39 (1954), 47–55.

Sarbin, Theodore R. "Role Theory," *Handbook of Social Psychology,* Vol. I. Reading, Mass.: Addison-Wesley, 1954.

Schmidhauser, John R. "Judicial Behavior and the Sectional Crisis of 1837–1860," *Journal of Politics,* 23 (November, 1961), 615–40.

——. "The Justices of the Supreme Court: A Collective Portrait," *Midwest Journal of Political Science,* 3 (February, 1959), 1–57.

——. "*Stare Decisis,* Dissent, and the Background of the Justices of the Supreme Court of the United States," *University of Toronto Law Journal,* 14 (1962), 194.

Schmidhauser, John R., and Gold, David. "Scaling Supreme Court Decisions in Relation to Social Background," *PROD,* 1 (May, 1958), 6–7.

Schubert, Glendon. "Bibliographical Essay: Behavioral Research in Public Law," *American Political Science Review,* 57 (June, 1963), 433–45.

——. "Civilian Control and *Stare Decisis* in the Warren Court," in Schubert (ed.), *Judicial Decision-Making.* New York: The Free Press of Glencoe, 1963.

——. "Judicial Attitudes and Voting Behavior: The 1961

Term of the United States Supreme Court," *Law and Contemporary Problems*, 28 (Winter, 1963), 100–42.

————. "Policy Without Law: An Extension of the Certiorari Game," *Stanford Law Review*, 14 (1962), 284.

————. "A Psychometric Model of the Supreme Court," *American Behavioral Scientist*, 5 (November, 1961), 14–18.

————. "From Public Law to Judicial Behavior." Introduction to Schubert (ed.), *Judicial Decision-Making*. New York: The Free Press of Glencoe, 1963.

————. "The 1960 Term of the Supreme Court: A Psychometric Analysis," *American Political Science Review*, 56 (March, 1962), 90–107.

Snyder, Eloise. "The Supreme Court as a Small Group," *Social Forces*, 36 (March, 1958), 232–38.

Snyder, Richard C. "A Decision-Making Approach to the Study of Political Phenomena," in Roland Young, (ed.), *Approaches to the Study of Politics*. Evanston: Northwestern University Press, 1958.

Sorauf, Frank. "Zorach v. Clauson: The Impact of a Supreme Court Decision," *American Political Science Review*, 53 (September, 1959), 777–91.

Spaeth, Harold J. "An Approach to the Study of Attitudinal Differences as an Aspect of Judicial Behavior," *Midwest Journal of Political Science*, 5 (May, 1961).

————. "Judicial Power as a Variable Motivating Supreme Court Behavior," *Midwest Journal of Political Science*, 6 (May, 1962, 54–82.

————. "The Judicial Restraint of Mr. Justice Frankfurter— Myth or Reality," *Midwest Journal of Political Science* 8 (February, 1964), 22–38.

————. "Unidimensionality and Item Variance in Judicial Scaling." Paper delivered at 1964 convention at the American Political Science Association, Chicago, Illinois.

Stover, Carl F. "Technology and the Law: A Look Ahead," *MULL* (March, 1963), 6–7.

Tanenhaus, Joseph. "Supreme Court Attitudes Toward Federal Administrative Agencies, 1947–56—An Application of Social

Science Methods to the Study of the Judicial Process," *Vanderbilt Law Review*, 14 (1961), 473.

Tate, Albert, Jr. "Judge as a Person," *Louisiana Law Review*, 19 (1959), 438.

_____. "'Policy' in Judicial Decisions," *Louisiana Law Review*, 20 (1959), 62.

Ulmer, S. Sidney. "Analysis of Behavior Patterns on the United States Supreme Court," *Journal of Politics*, 22 (November, 1960), 629–53.

_____. "Homeostatic Tendencies in the United States Supreme Court," in S. Sidney Ulmer (ed.), *Introductory Readings in Political Behavior* (Chicago: Rand McNally & Company, 1960). Pp. 167–88.

_____. "Leadership in the Michigan Supreme Court," in Glendon Schubert (ed.), *Judicial Decision-Making*. New York: The Free Press of Glencoe, 1963.

Vose, E. Clement. "Litigation as a Form of Pressure Group Activity," *Annals of the American Academy of Political and Social Science*, 319 (1958), 20–31.

Wechsler, Herbert. "Toward Neutral Principles of Constitutional Law," *Harvard Law Review*, 73 (1959), 1.

Cases

Baker v. *Carr* 369 U.S. 186 (1962)

Brown v. *Board of Education, Topeka* 349 U.S. 294 (1954)

Callopy v. *Newark Eye and Ear Infirmary* 27 N.J. 29 (1958)

Colegrove v. *Green* 328 U.S. 549 (1946)

Gomillion v. *Lightfoot* 364 U.S. 339 (1960)

Lochner v. *New York* 198 U.S. 45 (1905)

U.S. v. *Butler* 297 U.S. 1 (1936)

Youngstown Sheet and Tube Co. v. *Sawyer* 343 U.S. 579 (1951)

INDEX

PRINTED IN U.S.A.